Old Pubs
of
Sunderland

by

Alan Brett and John Royal

Black Cat Publications

First published in 1993
by
Black Cat Publications
163 Brandling Street
Roker
Sunderland
SR6 0LN

Proof Editor: Andrew Clark

ISBN 0 9518043 5 9

© Black Cat Publications

Printed by
Petersons
12 Laygate
South Shields
NE33 5RP

Picture Credits
Billy Bell
Margaret Calvert
John Lavelle
Newcastle Central Library
Rose Line Ltd.
Sunderland Antiquarian Society
Sunderland Central Library
(Local Studies Section)
Sunderland Echo
Sunderland Musuem
(Tyne and Wear Museums Service)
Sunderland Year Books
Tyne and Wear Archives Service
Vaux Group
Massie Wakinshaw

Special Thanks to
Harry Clark
Bobby Duckworth
John Gettings
Phil Hall
Peter Hepplewhite
Kevin Kernay
Edward O'Leary
Geoff Pearson
Martin Routledge
Ann Watt

Bibliography
C.H.G. Hopkins **Pallion 1874 to 1954: Church and People in a Shipyard Parish** 1954
Stuart Miller and Billy Bell **Sunderland in Old Photographs** 1991
William Mitchell Cranmer **History of Sunderland** 1919
Peter Gibson **Southwick on Wear** 1985
Taylor Potts **Sunderland: A History of the Town, Port, Trade and Commerce** 1892
William Robinson **The Story of the Royal Infirmary Sunderland** 1934
John Thompson **Old Monkwearmouth and its Surroundings: Seventy Years Ago** 1892
John Thompson **Recollections of the Four Hills on Monkwearmouth Shore and their Surroundings: Seventy Years Ago** 1891

Reports
F.M. Eden The State of the Poor (1797)
Robert Rawlinson Report to the General Board of Health on a Preliminary Inquiry as to the Sewerage, Drainage, Supply of Water and the Sanitary Condition of the Borough of Sunderland (1851)

Trade Directories
Burnett 1831
Christie 1871-72
Commercial 1820-22
Marwood Maritime 1854
Parson & White 1827
Pigot 1826
Vint & Carr 1844
Ward 1850 - 1937
Whellan 1865

Newspapers
Newcastle Courant
Sunderland Daily Echo
Sunderland Echo
Sunderland Weekly News
Sunderland Herald

Other Material
The Corder Manuscripts
Autobiography of Bernard Ogden (1769-1850)
Sunderland Council Minutes
Durham Marriage Bonds 1664-74

Early Days

Early Breweries

I do not propose to write an article on these as brewing, maltings and 'private home brewed' vats swarmed in Sunderland in the days when water was used to wash in and tea and coffee luxuries. There is nothing more surprising in the town than the number of inns ... beer shops wine and spirit merchants and the like; our ancestors must have literally swum in liquor.

James Corder 1867-1953

As a Quaker, Corder took a dim view towards suppliers of drink (which he deemed a 'social evil'). However, this did not stop other members of the Society of Friends from making fortunes from the beer trade. Names like Ogden and Burleigh were well known brewers in eighteenth and nineteenth century Sunderland. But the story of drink in Sunderland, and in Britain as a whole, went back much further. In the first century B.C., the Greek historian, Diodorus noted the diet of the British;

> Their food consisted chiefly of milk and venison. Their ordinary drink was water. Upon extraordinary occasions they drink a kind of fermented liquor made of barley, honey, or apples, and when intoxicated never failed to quarrel, like the ancient Thracians.

Two thousand years ago ale, mead and cider were all known to the inhabitants of these islands. As far as this area is concerned there is evidence of ale and wine on Wearside even before Sunderland existed.

The Venerable Bede (673-735) spent time in the monastery at St. Peter's, Monkwearmouth from the age of seven. He recorded the diet of a boy there. "He drank ale when he could get it, and water when he could not: wine was too dear." Bede also recorded dangers that could result from drink. He gave an account of an evil life of a monk. "He lived in a noble monastery (Jarrow), he lived ignobly ... He was much addicted to drunkenness and other vices."

In the seventeenth century, Durham Marriage Bonds* recorded a number of Sunderland brewers in the register:

1666 Francis Hall, Sunderland, beer brewer Bondsman to marriage of Kendall Sedgewick, Sunderland fitter and Mary Robinson 3rd February.
1672 William Robson Sunderland brewer married Elizabeth Hall 20th May.
1673 Hugh Ollivar Sunderland bearebrewer (sic) and Mary Chipchase both Sunderland 30th December.

* A bond was a statement by someone who knew the groom (or the groom himself) swearing there was no reason the marriage should not go ahead.

There are records of some of the inns at this time. These included: The Peacock, Golden Lion, Red Lion and The George. Some of these survived right through to this century. As Sunderland grew so did the number of drinking establishments. The town had one of the highest ratios of public houses to population in the country. In *The State of the Poor* (1797) Sir F.M. Eden reported 187 ale houses in Sunderland. This figure rose even higher until the middle of the last century. This was the peak of the drink trade. As the authorities gained greater control over licensed premises the number of pubs began to fall.

As for the Quakers, they still owned public houses in Sunderland well into this century. They did differ in some respects from ordinary proprietors, being more strict. On one occasion a man entering a Quaker-owned pub tripped on the step at the door and was refused service because the landlord said he was drunk.

A Vaux advert on the cover of a Sunderland AFC programme in the 1930s.

Welcome Tavern, Barrack Street

The old Welcome Tavern early in the century (*above*). Shortly before the First World War it was run by Tom Davison. Like many landlords at this time he also had a trade. When not running pubs he worked as an iron moulder in the North Eastern Engineering Works. The Welcome was pulled down and rebuilt in 1915. In the last century the Prussian Ship, Scotch Thistle and Friendly Tavern were all neighbours of the Welcome in Barrack Street. *Right:* The new pub in the 1930s when it still stood in a built-up area. Today, the Welcome is one of the few buildings, let alone pubs, to have survived in the area.

Regale Tavern, Hendon Road East
Left: The Regale Tavern in 1890. This is one of the oldest pubs in Sunderland, John Denton was landlord at the Regale 160 years ago. The present licensees are Tony and Audrey Joyce.

The Adelaide, Adelaide Place
In 1871 this pub was known as the Jack Crawford with Robert Ayre as landlord. In 1889, the owner, James Henderson closed the premises so improvements could be made. Work began on building a new front and digging a cellar. On the night of 2nd May, the lady living next door to the empty pub noticed a crack in the wall. She hurriedly removed her furniture fearing imminent collapse. At 9 p.m. her fears were realised when the whole of the shored-up building collapsed in a heap of rubble. After being rebuilt the name of the new pub was changed to The Adelaide after its location which itself had been named in honour of the wife of William IV.

Dock Hotel, Moor Terrace
As the name suggests a lot of this pub's trade came from the nearby Docks. During the nineteenth and early twentieth century Sunderland was one of the busiest ports in Britain. Sailors from both home and abroad gave the Dock Hotel a thriving trade.

West Country Arms, Mark Quay

This pub stood on Mark Quay on the East End riverside. Popular with sailors, it was known to regulars as 'The Marks'. Having stood since the early part of the nineteenth century, it fell into the river in 1886. Just prior to this, the manager, suspecting the foundations were unsafe, moved his premises to a house next door. Workmen had begun to demolish the building when a combination of high tides and swells brought the old pub tumbling down.

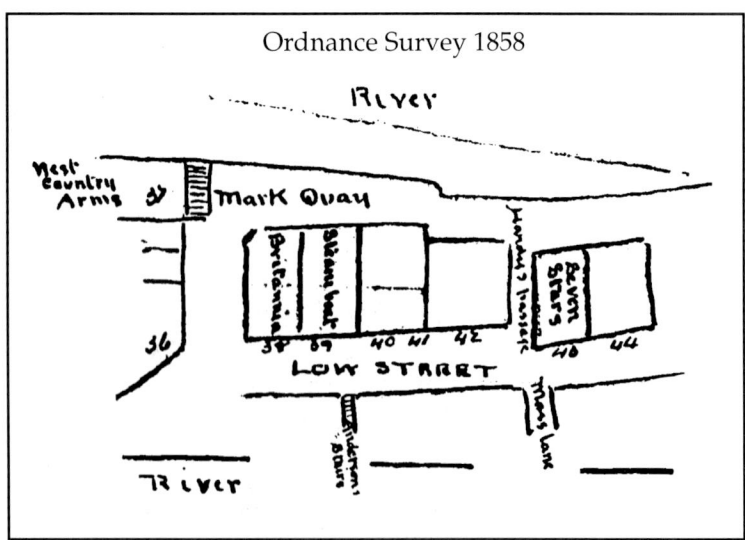

The West Country Arms in its new location survived only until 1894 when its licence was taken away. The reasons given were that the premises were unfit for business, the pub itself was not conducted in a proper and orderly manner and the owner was not a fit person to have a licence. At the 1894 Licensing Sessions the police objected to the renewal of the licence. Superintendent Huntley reported how men used to gather in Low Street beside the pub to fight, but he said they now went to the Town Moor. He also recalled his last visit there in August when it was "conspicuous for its very bad smell". Detective Inspector Purdy described the pub as a disorderly house, "frequented by thieves, prostitutes, sailors and 'all sorts' ". He himself had arrested thieves at the pub on two or three occasions. The licence was refused and the West Country Arms was closed.

A pub on the corner of Alma Street and Ogle Terrace, Southwick bore the same name, but this had gone by the end of the 1930s.

In the first half of the nineteenth century a public house licence on the riverside was worth its weight in gold to the owner. So when not one, but two licences were sacrificed, for other than ulterior motives, the event tended to be unique. James Everett *(above)*, a founder of the Methodist Free Church, was a man of high moral principles. Through his wife, Elizabeth Hutchinson, he inherited the Lynn Arms and Burton Coffee House on Thornhill Quay. Rather than make money on selling the licences he allowed them to lapse and the pubs were closed down.

Wharf Tavern, Black Bull Quay

Popular with sailors during the last century, the Wharf Tavern *(left of picture)* could not have been closer to the river. A letter from a Mr. Knott in the *Rawlinson Report* (1851) described how people risked life and limb on the riverside at this time. "There are some awkwardly situated public privies adjoining the river; four men have been drowned within a short space of time when going to these early in the morning, the lamps being out at the time."

Slipway Tavern, Thornhill Quay

On 13th May 1871, this riverside tavern was devastated by fire. The alarm was raised in the middle of the night by a passer-by, allowing the occupant, Mr. Griffiths and his wife and daughter to escape through an upstairs window. Despite widespread damage in both the bar and living quarters, the Slipway was refurbished and reopened for business. *Top left:* The Slipway Tavern in the middle of the last century when William Pearce was the landlord. *Top right:* The 1960s Slipway at Town End Farm, built in the days when there was still shipbuilding on the Wear.

Mariners' Arms, Custom House Quay

This was one of numerous East End riverside pubs. Its neighbours in the middle of the last century included: Whitwell Arms, Earl of Durham, Custom House Hotel, Yorkshire House, Marine Tavern, Honest Lawyer and Crown Inn.

Paddy's Goose, Low Street

In 1821 there were more than forty public houses in Low Street. The street's location along the riverside meant its pubs were especially popular with sailors and shipyard workers. Those trying to keep the peace in Low Street always had their hands full. On 5th March 1852 the *Sunderland Herald* reported two incidents at Paddy's Goose.

WAR IN PADDY'S GOOSE

Bryan Stafford, shipwright was charged by Mrs. Humble the landlady of Paddy's Goose, with having assaulted her. From the evidence it appeared that defendant being in a state of intoxication went to the complainant's house and held the door, refusing either to go in or come out, and at last he struck at the head of the landlady. Reprimanded and fined 5s and costs, or 14 days' imprisonment.

James Finnigan, packman was charged by Elizabeth Croft, with having assaulted her. From the evidence it appeared that the defendant went into Paddy's Goose, a public house in the Low-street, and opening his pack exposed his wares for sale. The servants in the house told him that the landlord did not allow hawkers to sell their goods in his house, on which the defendant flew into a passion, struck the complainant on the head with his box, and felled her on the floor. Reprimanded and fined 20s and costs, or one month's imprisonment.

As the century progressed the authorities clamped down on the bars in Low Street until there were only a handful left in 1900.

White Swan, High Street East
The White Swan lay above the old riverside houses in Low Street connected by narrow alleyways. 'Flattens' was just one of the characters who frequented this bar.

Royal Standard, High Street East
One of the Victorian bars that has survived in High Street East. Some of those that have disappeared include: Green Shutters, Atlas, Turk's Head and Edinburgh Castle.

White Lion, High Street East
Before James Martin took over the Golden Lion in 1762 he had been innkeeper of the White Lion. After being used as a warehouse for a number of years Hughie Quinn refurbished the building and reopened the White Lion in December 1988.

Clarendon Hotel, High Street East
This pub had a number of name changes in its early days. After it was rebuilt in 1818 it changed from the Hare and Hound to the Cropt Fox. Within four years it had become the Crown Inn and was later for a period a 'Board Inn' (with no sign). By 1865 it had the name Clarendon Hotel under which it is still going strong.

Golden Lion, High Street
This was one of Sunderland's oldest and most famous inns. In 1935 James Corder linked Sunderland's oldest deed with the Golden Lion.

> This property deed is dated 1296 - eighty years after the sealing of the Magna Carta. As an Elizabethan Survey of nearly 300 years later reported only 30 householders in the town, it is unlikely that there are now any other Sunderland deeds as early as 1296. It is probably the oldest Sunderland document of any kind.
>
> The property lay on the south side of High Street and extended to the Moor of the Bishop, this being the Hall Moor, south side of Coronation Street. It is probable that the "Golden Lion", the important coaching and family Inn - now rebuilt - stood on or about the site.
>
> A record of Bishop Hatfield, 1358, shows that the purchaser mentioned in the deed - John de le Schelis - had sold a property to John Hedworth. The only property on the south side of Coronation Street that can be traced to the latter's family, was sold in 1673 and later occupied by the "Golden Lion".
>
> Among the witnesses in 1296 was Robert the Bruce, Lord of Hartlepool, father of Robert the Bruce, King of Scotland, born 1274.

In 1755 a group of Freemasons met "at the sign of the Golden Lion". A famous early landlord was James Martin closely followed by Thomas Jowsey. The *Newcastle Courant* of 9th May 1795 reported "Married, Tuesday (5th), at Sunderland, Mr. Thomas Jowsey of the Golden Lion Inn, to Mrs. Reay, of the George Inn, in that place". Elizabeth Reay was the widow of the landlord of the George Inn and the couple took up residence there.

Sunderland-born Jack Casey, one of the greatest fighters never to win a British title. In the 1930s he trained at the Golden Lion.

At the 1890 Licensing Sessions the Chief Constable objected to the renewal of the Golden Lion's licence, on the grounds that a prize fight had taken place there on 20th May. Police had found a crowd watching two men fighting with gloves on in a ring. It was found out later these men were from Tyneside and were fighting for a £20 purse. Mr. Strachan, appearing for landlord, George Ovenden, told Magistrates:

> "It was a fair, good, English stand-up, one against the other ... I hope the time will come when every boy will be taught how to use his hands - when it will be part of the Board School education."

The Magistrates decided to renew the licence on the understanding that prize fighting did not continue. In the 1930s the Golden Lion was used again for boxing, Jack Casey trained at the pub during this period.

The Golden Lion was demolished in the 1960s, the carved golden lion from its frontage can now be seen above Sunderland Museum's Tea Room.

> **JOHN CHURCHILL,**
> Wine and Spirit Merchant,
> **JAMAICA VAULTS,**
> 33, HIGH STREET, SUNDERLAND.
>
> Fine London and Dublin Stout on Draught and in Bottles ; Burton, Bitter, and Sparkling Edinburgh and Masham Ales, of the Finest Quality, always on Draught.
>
> **SHIPS SUPPLIED.**

Jamaica Vaults, High Street East
This started life as an inn in 1847 when it was known as the British Oak. By 1853 it had the name Jamaica Vaults. Four years later John Churchill took over the Vaults, where he was to remain for the next three decades. During this time he built up the business into one of the town's most popular pubs. Every Christmas, Churchill helped the needy of the area by giving away large quantities of boiled beef, vegetables and bread. *Top left:* An advert for the Jamaica Vaults from *Ward's Directory* 1859-60. The aging building was knocked down and the Black Cat built on the site in the 1960s. This later became The Eastender which it remains today *(top right)*.

Saddle Inn, High Street East
Martin Stephenson bought this inn in 1777 and as he was also a saddler this would account for its name. The old Sunderland custom of perambulating the parish boundaries ended at Mrs. Davison's Saddle Inn on 3rd May 1853, where dinner was taken by the dignitaries. Around the time of the First World War the Saddle Inn was closed as redundant and stood derelict for a number of years.

Holy Island Castle, Coronation Street
In the last century a number of Sunderland pubs had the name of Northumberland castles. As well as the Holy Island Castle there was the Tynemouth Castle in Stafford Street and in Lombard Street there was the Bamborough Castle and the Alnwick Castle.

Bridge Hotel, High Street West

This coaching inn was converted from the eighteenth century Sunderland residence of the Lambton Family. This happened shortly after 1796, the year the bridge over the Wear was built. An advert for the Bridge Hotel from this time (*below*).

John Donkin took over in the 1840s further building up the hotel's reputation (*right*).

The Bridge Hotel was the starting point for The Royal Mail coach to York and The Union coach to Whitby. The Lambtons maintained their links with The Bridge by making it their headquarters when in town. This was sometimes at the hotel's cost as, on one occasion after John George Lambton addressed a crowd in Sunderland, a mob smashed the Bridge's windows. The Bridge Hotel is still open today (*below*), having lost some of its former glory with the movement of the town centre westward.

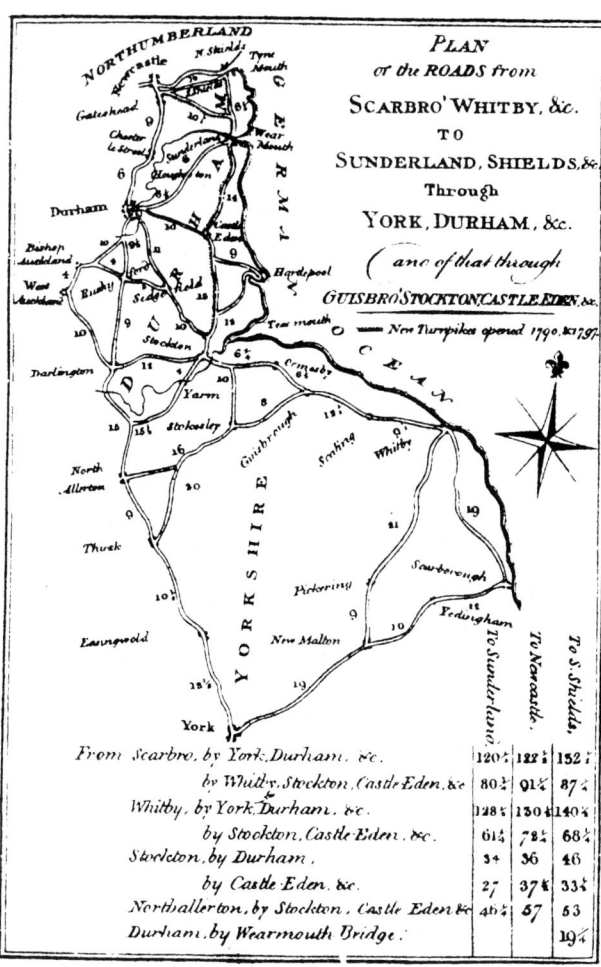

Eagle Tavern, High Street East
There was an inn on this site as far back as 1674 when John Groves ran the Three Crowns. This later became the Exchange Tavern and in the 1850s the Royal Exchange. At this time the landlord was a Mr. Metcalfe, who also acquired the deserted Corn Exchange Chapel next door and ran 'musical entertainments' there. After this failed in 1863 both buildings were taken over by Mr. Newbigin, who set about rebuilding, forming the Eagle Tavern and the Eagle Tobacco Factory (*above*). At this time a 6' 6" high pine Golden Eagle stood on the top of the building. After this was taken down it stood in a yard in Deptford (*bottom left*). Today, it is believed to be in Jersey. Before the First World War, Fairgrieves took over the building and shortly afterwards the Eagle Tavern closed. The building still stands today, with the same company of electrical engineers in business there (*bottom right*).

Half Moon Inn, High Street East
Left: This inn had been converted from a private residence in the eighteenth century. In 1801 the Half Moon had its windows broken in a riot over the price of corn. In 1903 plans were drawn up and the pub was rebuilt, which included an 'exaggerated baroque' frontage. After lying derelict for many years the Half Moon was demolished but not before the Edwardian facade had been shipped to the United States.

British Empire, High Street East
Right: The British Empire was housed in what was originally Horner's Commercial Hotel - The Thompson Arms. Built in 1840 on a site adjoining the Exchange Building, the 'North Briton Coach' left here for Durham each morning, returning in the evening. The hotel, however, was not a success and it closed after a few years. The premises were than sub-let into shops and a public house. The British Empire occupied part of the building for over a century. After standing derelict for a number of years the British Empire was torn down in 1973.

Grey Horse, High Street East
Left: This old pub stood two doors up from the Eagle Tavern. In the eighteenth century it was known as the Cock Inn, having been shortened from the Fighting Cock Inn, suggesting there was a cock pit nearby. By 1808 it had become known as the Grey Horse which it remained until its closure in the 1930s.

Ship Inn, High Street East

At one time there was more than one Ship Inn in Sunderland. *Left:* The Ship Inn at No. 1 High Street East during the early 1880s was owned by Robert Bowey Lutert. At one time a room in the pub was reserved for ships' captains, with no lower ratings allowed in. A new Ship Inn was built on the site and is now called the Corner House *(above)*.

Boar's Head, High Street East

The 1930s clearances for the New Quay demolished all the buildings surrounding the Boar's Head except the pub itself. There has been an inn on the site since the eighteenth century. By 1827 it was known as the Masons' Arms. In 1834 it had become the Boar's Head which it remains to this day *(left)*.

Lord Byron, Maling's Rigg

This public house was unusual in that its upstairs room had formerly been used as a masonic lodge, a place of worship and a sparring saloon. In 1814 the Unitarians converted an old Freemasons' Lodge into a chapel. The Unitarians left in 1830 for a new chapel in Bridge Street. It later became a sparring saloon run by George Craggs. One noted visitor to this establishment was bareknuckle prizefighter James 'Deaf' Burke.

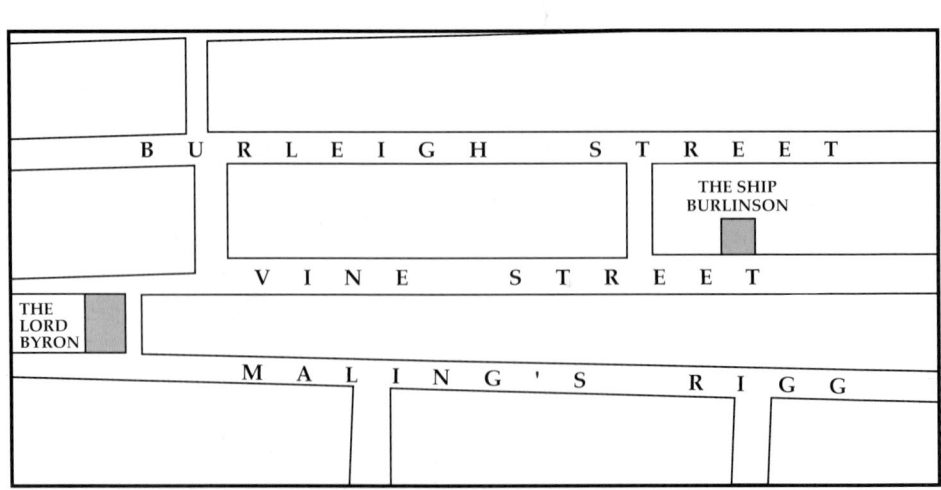

'The Deaf 'un' had become Champion of England by beating Simon Byrne in a gruelling three hour fight in 1833. Three days later Byrne died and Burke was charged with causing his death, but was found not guilty at his trial.

In 1903 the Chief Constable opposed the renewal of the licence of the nearby Ship Burlinson. This public house and the Lord Byron both had the same owners and they indicated to the Magistrates they would surrender the licence of the Lord Byron if opposition to the Ship Burlinson was dropped. The Bench agreed to this and the eventful life of the Lord Byron came to a close.

Market Hotel, Coronation Street

Right: Before becoming a pub the Market Hotel had been the home of John Thornhill (after whom the district in Sunderland is named). The Market and its neighbour, the Butchers' Arms took their names from the numerous slaughterhouses and markets in the area. In the middle of the last century within a hundred yards of the Market Hotel there were half a dozen different types of market. There were fish, meat, old clothes, earthenware, boot and shoe and fruit and vegetable markets. As well as the Market Hotel there was also the Market Tavern in Church Street.

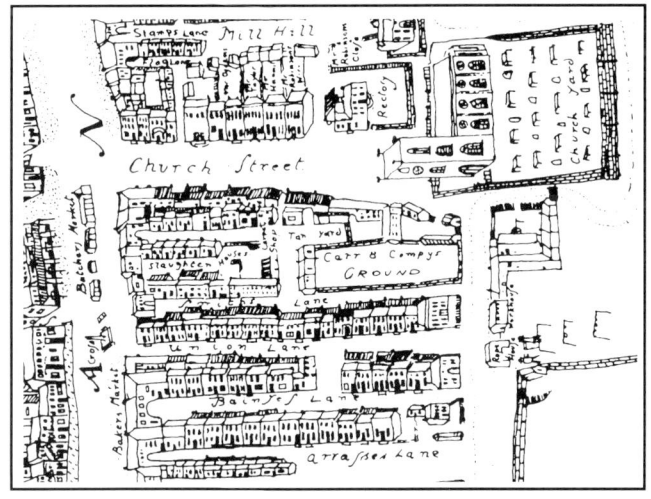

The area in which the Market Hotel and the Butchers' Arms stood used to be known as the Shambles. From as early as 1691 there were slaughterhouses there. A hundred years later these can be seen on Rain's Eye Plan *(left)* along with butchers' and bakers' markets.

Butchers' Arms, Coronation Street

James Corder recalls how butchers were an influential group in the eighteenth century. In 1724 at the races on the Town Moor there was a special event for butchers' horses. A new covered market was built nearby and in 1831 this housed 61 butchers' shops. Therefore, it is not surprising that the Butchers' Arms was so named. In the 1950s, Jimmy Bell and Peggy Scott ran the pub. Like the Market Hotel this has been demolished.

Attitudes to Drink

Today, we view alcohol as a luxury but in the past it was seen as a necessity. At the end of the eighteenth and early nineteenth century Sunderland's water supply was provided by a number of deep wells. Many of these became polluted, helping to spread disease such as typhoid and cholera through the rapidly increasing population.

People in Sunderland as in other crowded large towns turned to safer 'thirst quenches'. While boiling water did make it safe, coffee and tea were expensive. Milk, before the days of pasteurisation and refrigeration was a dangerous drink. Therefore, beer and spirits provided a cheap, safe and readily available source of refreshment.

Up to the 1860s alcohol was used in hospitals both as an anaesthetic and medicine. In *The Story of the Royal Infirmary Sunderland*, William Robinson recalled how during this period nearly everyone in hospital took some form of daily alcohol.

**Sunderland Infirmary
Table of Diet 1823**

Common Diet -Beer, *every day*, a child of 5-8 years, 4 oz; 8-12 years, 10oz; 12-16 years, 12 oz; and over 16 years, 1 pint.
Low Diet -Beer not more than 1 pt. a day.

Alcohol even became part of the diet in the Workhouse, until this too was phased out, not least by public pressure. The *Sunderland Herald* of 19th May 1843 reported;

AN ASTOUNDING FACT
**A return was yesterday laid before the guardians of the Sunderland Union, which stated that the amount expended in wine and spirits, from Dec., 1841, to Dec., 1842, for the use of persons in the workhouse is £36 0s 3d. The items are as follows:-
Ale, £9 19s 11d; Gin £5 18s 10d; Brandy, 10s 6d; Wine £19 11s. We do not know whether any explanation has been given relative to this large expenditure, but certainly it requires explanation.**

In 1873 the Board of Guardians voted 13 to 10 against allowing the inmates of the Workhouse a glass of beer on Christmas Day. One member pointed out that beer had probably been the reason most inmates found themselves in the Workhouse.

For many workers, alcohol was seen as a necessity, especially in jobs that required hard physical labour, such as foundry work, building work and farming at harvest time. The Government even recognised alcohol had a place in the services. The rum ration to sailors continued right into the 1970s.

The public house often played an important role to groups of workmen. Apart from seeking entertainment after a long voyage at sea, pubs were often the place ships' crews were paid off. Which in turn meant they had plenty of money to go straight on a drinking session.

In the days of 'jobbing work' in the shipyards, different squads of tradesmen met in pubs to share out their pay.

NOURISHING AND SUSTAINING.

WM. ST. JOHN'S

Invalid Oatmeal Stout

Strongly Recommended by the Medical Faculty
for Invalids.

It has been analysed by Sir Chas. A. Cameron, Professor of Chemistry, Royal College of Surgeons, Ireland, who reports :—

"I have analysed a specimen of Oatmeal Stout submitted to me for that purpose by Messrs. Wm. St. John, Queen Street Brewery, Sunderland,

Alcohol 7·82
100 parts contain ... Malt Extract 7·70
Including Albuminoids ·22

The proportions of **ALCOHOL** and **MALT EXTRACT** are equal to the proportions occurring in the **HIGH-CLASS STOUTS**."

(*Signed*) SIR CHAS. A. CAMERON, C.B., M.D., F.R.C.P., F.R.C.S., F.I.C.
Professor of Chemistry, Royal College of Surgeons, Ireland.

To be obtained from—

WM. ST. JOHN,
Brewer, Wine and Spirit Merchant,
Offices: 5, NORFOLK STREET, SUNDERLAND.
NAT. TEL. No. 68.

An advert from 1905 recommending stout for invalids.

Platers, riveters, burners and others, would meet to share out their earnings to their labourers. These 'black squads' would inevitably go on the drink to celebrate. The term to go on a 'black 'un' is still used today when men stop out drinking after work.

Launch day became a traditional time for a drinking session for shipyard workers. On 18th July 1856, the *Sunderland Herald* reported:

AFTER THE LAUNCH
William Dinning, beerhouse-keeper, Southwick, was charged with having his house open at a quarter to one o'clock on the morning of 21st *ult*. The officer found a number of drunken men inside, but it appeared that no drink had been filled after ten o'clock. The company were all shipwrights, who had been keeping it up after a launch, and the landlord, to clear the house, had "stopped the music and withdrew the fiddler several times", but he always got in again. Fined 30s.

Alcohol was also an important factor in the 'rite of passage'. In the 1910 *Sunderland Year Book*, James Spencer recalled 'An East End Christening'. "In accordance with old Sunderland custom it (the baby) was taken first of all to church and christened and then to the house of its oldest available relative." Then the father and grandfather "armed with big jugs, repaired to the public house at the corner, and returned with the jugs filled with 'mixed'." The tradition of 'wetting the baby's head' persists to this day, while other traditions, like wakes have become less popular. These have been replaced with such celebrations as stag and hen nights, birthdays and anniversaries.

Royal Hotel, Prospect Row
At the Licensing Sessions on 4th February 1932 the licence for the Royal Hotel was not renewed and the pub was referred for compensation. Although The Royal dated from the middle of the nineteenth century, it had been rebuilt only twenty years before. In March 1933 Reverend Edgar Jackson bought the redundant pub *(left)* to replace St. John's Settlement. The vicar had gone out on a limb when the property became available, and bought it with his own money. The Charity Commissioners supported his actions and hoped to raise the money from the sale of the old mission which had to be cleared for the building of the new Deep Water Quay.

Germania Inn, High Street East
At the end of the last century Carl Senstius kept this inn, which appears to have been named in honour of his homeland. The popularity of lager among today's drinkers is surprisingly not a new phenomenon. Senstius, who was also a shipbroker, imported lager to Sunderland one hundred years ago.

Station Hotel, Prospect Row
The railway line from Durham built in the 1830s terminated at the staiths in Low Quay. The railway station stood near the Town Moor and it was after this wooden structure the pub was named. The Station Hotel was known to locals as 'Hutchies', after the Hutchinson family who ran the pub from the 1880s through to the Second World War. After over a century in business the Station Hotel closed and was demolished in 1965.

Globe Hotel, High Street East
In the 1790s when this pub was known as The Fountain, a cockpit stood at the back. By 1827 it was known as the Gardener's Tavern until becoming The Globe in the middle of the last century.

Smyrna Hotel, South Durham Street
Like most nineteenth century pubs sawdust was the floor covering of the Smyrna bar. Long before the days of wall to wall carpeting, sawdust from the numerous local sawmills, was the standard pub floor covering.

Waterman's Tavern, Hat Case
The Waterman's Tavern stood in an area known as the Hat Case. This crowded part of the East End was surrounded by pubs in the last century. There was the Holyrood Hotel in Warren Street, Sir Colin Campbell, Riggers' Arms and Cross Keys in High Street East and Paul Pry and Oak Tavern in Silver Street. Work began to clear the slums in the Hat Case in the 1890s. When Harrison's Buildings was erected on the site in 1903, the Waterman's Tavern was one of the few buildings to survive.

> In 1834 Abigail Luckly was landlady at the Life Boat, Pottery Bank. This was one of three Life Boat public houses in Sunderland. In the same year there were also six Noah's Arks, six Royal Oaks (one at Hylton) and five Wheatsheafs.

Norfolk House, Norfolk Street
In 1893 George William Chipperfield was landlord of the Norfolk House. *Above left:* The side entrance to the pub in the 1960s. The Norfolk House closed as a pub around 1970 but was then used as a Merchant Navy club for a number of years. The building still stands today and is used as a business premises *(above right)*.

Villiers Hotel, Villiers Street

When this pub first opened, Villiers Street was one of the town's most fashionable streets. As the town centre moved westward the area became less popular.

Top: An all-male outing setting off from The Villiers in the early part of the century.

In 1902 The Villiers was just one of a dozen pubs in Sunderland owned by John Vipond (*left*).

The Villiers is no longer a pub but the building still stands today (*right*).

John Vipond,
ALE, WINE, and = =
= SPIRIT MERCHANT.

VILLIERS HOTEL	VILLIERS STREET
WHITE LION HOTEL	HIGH STREET EAST
CROWN & THISTLE HOTEL	,, ,, ,,
PILOT HOTEL	,, ,, ,,
FISHERMAN'S ARMS	BURLEIGH STREET
ROBBIE BURNS' ARMS	CORONATION STREET
ALMA HOTEL	RAILWAY STREET
TEMPLE BAR	JOHNSON STREET
LAMP TAVERN, SILKWORTH ROW, HIGH ST. WEST	
GLASSMAKERS' ARMS	TRIMDON STREET
CALEDONIAN ARMS	,, ,,
CROWTREE INN (on & after Jan. 16,'02)	CROWTREE ROAD
BARCLAY STREET STORES	
AND	
PRINCE OF WALES' HOTEL, UNION STREET,	NORTH SHIELDS

Only Ales, Wines, Spirits, and Cigars of the best quality
ARE SUPPLIED.

Proprietor - JOHN VIPOND, Villiers Hotel

Hendon Station Hotel, Hendon Road
The Hendon Station took its name from the railway station that stood opposite. This station replaced the Town Moor station in 1858 and was in turn replaced.

Waverley Hotel, Norman Street
This Hendon pub was run by John Wharton in 1871. Its more famous namesake stood opposite the Central Station in High Street West.

Three Tuns, Moor Street
One of the busiest times for pubs like the Three Tuns (*left*) was during the East End Carnival. The nearby Royal Hotel in Prospect Row used to employ a man to stay down in the cellar all day to change the barrels over when the carnival was on.

Left: The street corner on which the Three Tuns stood. At one time in some areas of town almost every street corner had a pub on it.

Lord Roberts, Winchester Terrace
Built in 1900, the Lord Roberts took its name from the popular British commander in the Boer War. This year had proved a turning point in the war, with the relief of Mafeking and Kimberley. Sunderland also later recognised these events by naming streets in town in their honour.

In the 1860s, wine and spirit merchant, James Brett ran a 'Board' Inn in High Street East. This was an inn with no sign i.e. no name. This was not an uncommon practice, in 1827 there were 15 Board inns in Sunderland. The Board Inn on Durham Road is an example today of how it has survived to became a pub name in itself.

Linden Arms, Linden Place
In March 1971 the Linden Arms was knocked down by mistake! As the Council and the Whitbread Brewery were negotiating over the future of the empty pub, contractors believing (wrongly) the Linden Arms was in the Ward Street Compulsory Purchase Area, went ahead and demolished the building. All that was left for the Brewery to do was to seek £1,400 compensation for its loss.

Bush Inn, Ward Street
Above left: The old Bush Inn on the end of a terrace of houses. Redevelopment in this part of Hendon claimed a large number of public houses. *Above right:* Although left standing on its own, the Bush is one of those that have survived.

Nat. Tel. 1614.

PETER DUFFY,
SUNDERLAND,

Wine and Spirit Merchant.

Britannia Inn,	Trimmers' Arms,
George Street, Monkwearmouth.	Pemberton Street, Hendon.
The Neptune Hotel,	Glassmakers' Arms,
Pilgrim Street, Monkwearmouth.	Johnson Street, Bishopwearmouth.

AND THE FULLY LICENSED

Square and Compass, Cornforth.

ALL ENTIRELY FREE.

HIGHEST QUALITY EDINBURGH & BURTON ALES.
CHOICE CIGARS.

Private Address :—42, BRIGHT STREET, MONKWEARMOUTH.

Trimmers' Arms, Pemberton Street
The Trimmers' Arms was one of the pubs owned by Peter Duffy in 1910. *Left*: An advert for Duffy's other pubs in Sunderland

Oddfellows Arms, Robinson Terrace
In the early part of this century the Oddfellows was owned by Horatio Stratton. His grandson was the famous Sunderland footballer Horatio 'Raich' Stratton Carter.

The Divan, Hendon Road
In the 1930s this was known as the 'Little House' after landlord, Tommy Little. At this time he ran trips to Sunderland's away matches.

The Salutation, Hendon Road
In 1865 John Ramshaw was the Salutation's landlord. A century later, like its neighbours the Hendon Hotel, New Shades and White House Hotel, the Salutation was gone.

The Wheatsheaf, Moor Street
The Wheatsheaf is one of the oldest surviving pubs in Sunderland, in 1820 Edward Grimes was the landlord. *Above:* A wintery scene of the Wheatsheaf in the 1960s, with Holy Trinity Church in the background.

> **Wellington Vaults, High Street East**
> In the middle of the last century this was known to locals as 'The Rum Running House'. It was said there was a tunnel running to Low Quay which was used for smuggling spirits. On 14th August 1883 a gas explosion ripped through, what was called, the Wellington Hotel. One room was severely damaged, windows were shattered and walls cracked and scorched. The daughter of the landlady, had struck a match to light a gas lamp but this ignited a gas leak. The girl was fortunate to 'only' have her arms scorched and hair burnt off. A man in the bar at the time was flung from one end of the room to the other. His injuries were limited to 'shock to the system'.

Hendon Grange Hotel, Ocean Road East
In the early years of the nineteenth century before Hendon began to develop there stood a farm house called Hendon Grange. The pub that bears its name stands on the southern border of Sunderland overlooking the sea. Its address in Ocean Road, refers to the German Ocean, the former name of the North Sea.

Blue House, Commercial Road
There was a Blue House public house in Hendon in the middle of the last century. The nearby Blue House Field was Sunderland Football Club's first ground in 1879. In 1898 the pub was put up for sale with the "option or privilege of building within 12 months a hotel on a new free site at the corner of Corporation Road and Commercial Road in substitution for the present site of the Blue House Inn". *Above:* The Blue House today.

Laburnum Cottage, Robinson Terrace
Above: The old Laburnum between the wars. The rebuilt Laburnum Cottage in the 1950s *(right)*.

Licensing

In March 1993, Home Secretary, Kenneth Clarke, proposed changing the licensing laws allowing children of all ages into public houses. At one time there were no restrictions on children in pubs. Landlords in the last century even encouraged the sale of alcohol to children by offering tiny glasses of gin known as 'squibs'. Children as young as five were employed in factories and mines and it was not until 1819 that legislation limited children to a '12 hour day'. The 1908 Children's Act made it illegal for anyone under 14 to go into a pub. Prior to this women could take their babies and children into pubs *(below)*. In 1923 the drinking age in pubs was raised to the present 18 years.

The major effect on the licensing trade as a whole took place in 1830 with the passing of the Duke Of Wellington's Sale of Beer Act. Up to that time the sale of alcohol was strictly controlled by Licensing Magistrates. The new Act broke down barriers by allowing any householder to sell beer for a two guinea fee. Beershops rapidly spread throughout the country from 24,000 in 1830 to 46,000 six years later. The 1869 Wine and Beerhouse Act stemmed this flood of beerhouses, which at this time numbered 53,000. The Act gave the Magistrates the sole right to grant licences. This put the opening of new pubs back under the control of the Magistrates. However, the Act was not retrospective and existing beerhouses could not be refused a licence (except in exceptional circumstances).

The next major shake up of the Licensing Laws occurred during the First World War. The wartime Government feared the consequences drinking would have on key industries, such as munitions factories and shipyards. In March 1915, Prime Minister, Lloyd George declared, "We are fighting Germany, Austria and drink and the greatest of these deadly foes is drink".

Legislation was passed which reduced opening hours and diluted the strength of beer. Afternoon closing was introduced thus ending all day opening. The restrictions had the desired effect, alcohol consumption was reduced from 89 million gallons in 1914 to 37 million gallons in the last year of the war. In 1921 the temporary restrictions imposed during the war were made permanent.

At every opportunity the police attempted to reduce the number of licensed premises at least to the pre 1830 levels. At the Annual Licensing (Brewster) Sessions police produced their 'black list' of those they opposed the renewal of their licence. These were licensees who had

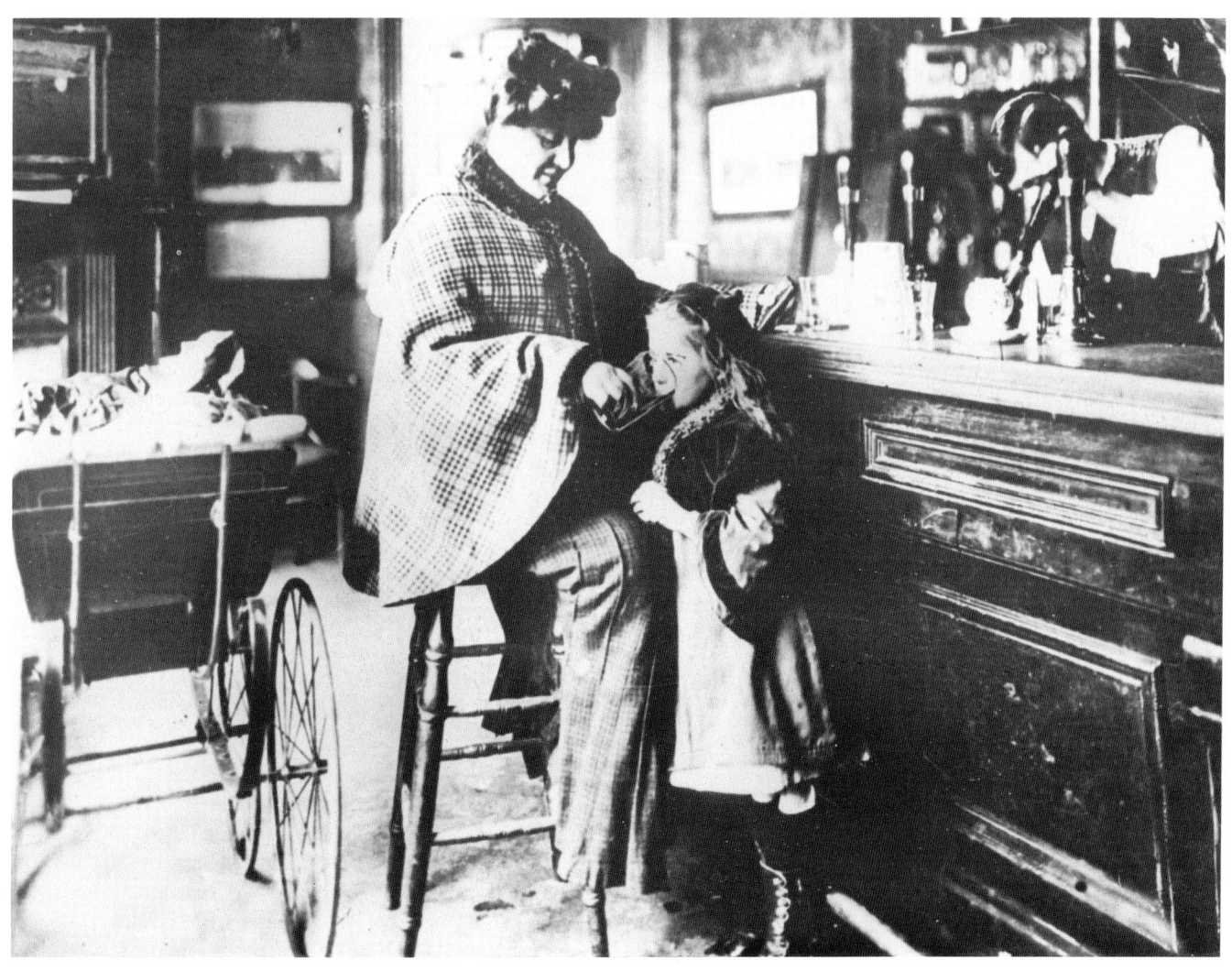

been found guilty of offences during the previous year.

At the 1894 Brewster Sessions in August and September the Chief Constable opposed the renewal of licenses to:

Crown and Sceptre, Mill Lane, Hylton Road - not the same premises as licensed.
Cross Keys, North Quay - ordered to pay costs 8th September 1893 for selling drink during prohibited hours
Plough Inn. Low Row - Fined 40s on 8th November 1893 for selling intoxicating drinks to a drunken person
Newcastle Arms, Millum Terrace - not in a sanitary condition
West Country Arms, Mark Quay - premises unfit for carrying on business, were not conducted in a proper and orderly manner and the applicant was not a fit person to have a licence.
Beerhouse, Howard Street - not the same premises as licensed

There were also new applications for a provisional licence for a new **Blue Bell**, Roker Avenue, **The Shades**, High Street East and two 'off' licences.

The Licensing Magistrates rejected the applications of the West Country Arms, Cross Keys, Blue Bell and The Shades. They renewed the licences of the Crown and Sceptre, Plough Inn and the Beerhouse in Howard Street. The police withdrew their objection to the Newcastle Arms.

The Annual Returns for 1894 reported there were 561 licences existing in Sunderland. These comprised; Licensed Victuallers for consumption on and off the premises (243), beerhouses and wine houses (170), beerhouses 'off' (124), dealers' retail licences 'off' (7), and wholesale spirits and wines (17).

The number of licences reported to have been refused and surrendered between 1874 and 1894 was 133 and the number of new licences granted in the same period was 18.

NOTICE.

WE, the undersigned Magistrates, do hereby warn and caution all Publicans and Retailers of Spirits not to allow or permit their Houses to be opened on New-Year's-Day. And we hereby give notice, that we have given positive directions to the Constables to give information against all Persons who may offend against the tenor of their Licences.

G. ROBINSON,
A. FENWICK,
J. D. GARTHWAITE,
S. EDEN,
THOS. WILKINSON.

Justice Room, Sunderland,
31st Dec. 1831.

SUNDERLAND: PRINTED BY REED & SON.

A warning from Sunderland Magistrates not to open on New Year's Day 1832. At the time the town was ravaged by cholera and drink was thought to weaken the body's defences against the disease.

The Rink, Hudson Road
Above: The Rink in the 1970s. After being in business for a hundred years the Rink changed to its present name of Strokes.

Windsor Castle, Nile Street
This pub used to be called the Post Office (the Old General Post Office) is nearby. It is still a popular watering hole for postmen after work. A pub called the Windsor Castle stood in Zetland Street at the turn of the century.

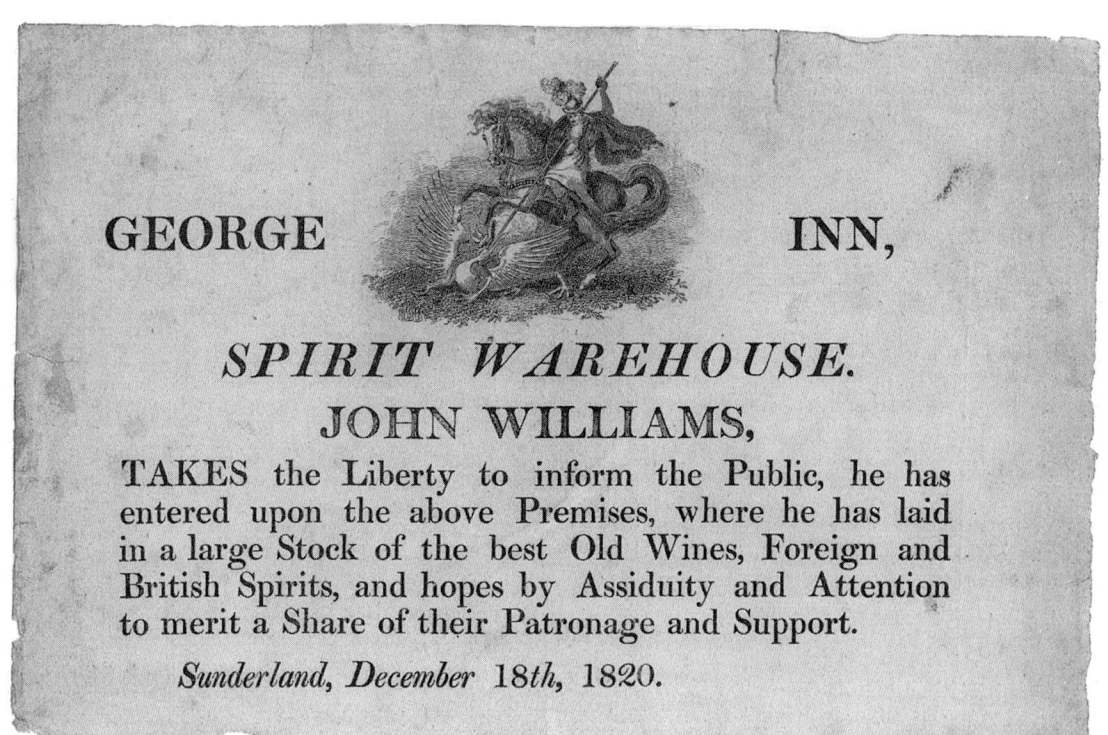

George Inn, High Street East
This was one of the main coaching inns in Sunderland during the eighteenth century. In 1783 the Phoenix Lodge of the Freemasons used to meet in a room at the Inn. In his autobiography, Bernard Ogden recalled the George Inn during the 1780s. While serving a seven year apprenticeship with a druggist Ogden recorded how he had been in danger of acquiring many bad habits. A fellow shop worker, George Eastman, "was anything but a desirable companion for a young man. Uneducated and fond of low company, he was never so happy as when amidst the waiters and post boys of the George Inn, which was next door to us". At the time the George Inn was also the headquarters of the military stationed in the town.

Hendon Hotel, Hendon Road
This was one of many pubs on Hendon Road, in the days when it was a bustling thoroughfare. Part of the road was formerly called Cutty Throat Lonnin reflecting a more sinister past.

The Alexandra, Queen Alexandra Road
Above: The Alexandra in the 1950s. In 1985 the Alexandra was redeveloped into a 'fun pub' and renamed the Porcupine Park. It has recently undergone another renovation, this time back to a traditional pub style, accompanied by a return to its original name.

Old Bull and Dog, High Street East
The name of this pub recalls the days when bull baiting took place on the Town Moor and Bishopwearmouth Green. In the 1820s John Barron was the landlord of the Old Bull and Dog. Barron was also a butcher and his shop was next to the pub. Later in the century it was closed as redundant and was then used as a lodging house. *Below:* An advert from the 1859-60 *Ward's Directory*.

```
         H. T. BARRY,
WINE, SPIRIT, ALE & PORTER MERCHANT,
          OLD BULL AND DOG INN,
    42, HIGH STREET, SUNDERLAND.

  Aitchison & Co.'s Celebrated Sparkling Scotch Ales.
BASS & CO.'S BURTON & PALE ALES, on Draught and in Bottles.
   LONDON AND DUBLIN STOUT.—SHIPS SUPPLIED.
```

Tatham Arms, Tatham Street
Right: This pub was named after the street in which it stood, which in turn was named after an old Sunderland family.

Parade Arms, The Parade

In 1936 a new Parade was built to replace the existing nineteenth century public house. In 1962 the Parade Arms stood in splendid isolation after neighbouring streets had been demolished in the slum clearances *(top left)*. The Parade survived and today factories have taken the place of houses as its neighbours *(top right)*.

American Hotel, Barrack Street

Right: The bar in the American Hotel at the turn of the century. Only one customer braves the camera, the others have left their beer standing on the bar. The hand operated bar pumps were first used early last century, prior to their introduction ale had to be carried from the cellar in jugs or served from barrels behind the bar. The American bar had both bar pumps and the barrels.

International Hotel, International Road

Left: The International had formerly been Hendon House, home of the Bramwell family. Christopher Bramwell had established a brewery in Burdon Lane in 1769. Later the Wear Brewery opened in Chester Road. The Bramwells owned a large amount of land in Hendon and a number of streets bore the family's names, such as Bramwell Road, Henry Street, Mabel Terrace and Addison Street. The old house was converted into a hotel in the middle of the last century. The International was known to locals as the Nash.

The Londonderry, Surtees Street
This old pub stood on the corner of Surtees Street and Page Street in Hendon. Like the Londonderry Hotel in High Street West, it was named after local landowner, the Marquis of Londonderry.

Alma Hotel, Railway Street
At one time there were a number of pubs in Sunderland called the Alma. The first appeared around 1855 in Church Street, within a year there was another Alma in High Street. This suggests the name came from the Battle of the Alma, the first British victory in the Crimean War in September 1854. The Alma Hotel on the corner of Railway Street and Clark Street dates from a couple of years later.

Excelsior Hotel, Lawrence Street
In 1910 when this beerhouse was put up for sale it comprised a bar and sitting room and covered quoit ground at the rear. At this time it held an ale, porter and tobacco licence. Two views showing the Excelsior, in the 1950s *(above)* and more recently *(right)*.

Queen's Hotel, Hendon Road

The old Queen's Hotel *(above)* was known to locals as Charltons after one of its former owners. After the pub was demolished in the early 1960s a new Queen's was built on the site. In 1981 the new landlord, Tommy Cooper, changed the pub's name to The Charltons *(left)*. His former job was in demolition and one of the buildings he had knocked down was the original Queen's Hotel.

The Salem, Salem Street

The Salem is now known as the Tap and Spile *(right)*, but the present building only dates from the 1930s. The original Salem is much older, dating from the last century. In 1898 the pub was one of a number of properties belonging to Abel Chapman that were sold to Camerons Breweries.

The Rosedene, Queen Alexandra Road

Rosedene House was built in the last century as a family mansion in its own grounds. In 1961 after standing empty for a decade, the council agreed to plans to convert the building to a public house. On 6th May 1964 The Rosedene opened its doors for the first time. The Rosedene today *(right)*. There are plans for the pub to be renovated in late 1993. Part of the £400,000 cost of the work will go on providing better access for the disabled.

The Borough, Vine Place
The Borough took its name from the granting of borough status to the town. A parallel was seen recently when city status was granted to Sunderland and The Beehive reopened as The New City.

Above: The sign of the New City (formerly The Beehive). In 1809 an Act of Parliament was passed for improving the town of Sunderland. Commissioners were appointed with powers "for removing nuisances, paving, lighting, and otherwise improving the town". The commissioners ordered the removal of pub signs that protruded too far into the street. Local poet, Peter Flint lamented their actions in verse:

> Wolfe* and Nelson** hide their face,
> Our mighty heroes they disgrace,
> Transfixed against the wall.

* General Wolfe, High Street East.
** Lord Nelson, Low Street.

STRAWBERRY COTTAGE
TEA AND PLEASURE GARDENS,
TUNSTALL LANE, BISHOPWEARMOUTH.

W. FARROW has the pleasure to announce to the inhabitants of Sunderland and the surrounding neighbourhood, that he has just completed extensive alterations and improvements in the above Gardens, and that they are now open for the Summer Season, with a most promising supply of FRUITS and FLOWERS, of the choicest kind the locality is capable of producing, and especially STRAWBERRIES, for the cultivation of which these gardens have so long been celebrated.

W. F. particularly invites his friends to avail themselves of the wholesome air these gardens afford, and acquaints them that excellent TEA, SPICE CAKES, &c. will be provided at One Shilling per head, and all other refreshments at a very moderate charge.

Spirits, Bottled Stout, Ale, Porter, Cigars, &c.

The summit of Tunstall Hill affords by far the most beautiful Marine and Landscape Scenery that this neighbourhood can present to the eye, and its salubrious air cannot fail to benefit those who may avail themselves of it.

Strawberry Cottage is situated at the foot of this fine eminence, and will be found a convenient resting place for parties going to or returning therefrom.

For the kind support given to Strawberry Cottage and Gardens, during the last thirteen years, W. F. returns sincere thanks, and hopes that the great improvements he has made in his House and Gardens will secure to him a continuance and extension thereof.

Strawberry Cottage, Strawberry Gardens,
Above left: This inn, which stood at the bottom of Strawberry Bank, dated from the early part of the last century. An advert from 1844 (*above right*) shows the pub was not the only attraction drawing people to visit Strawberry Gardens. The landlord in 1856, Robert Fair was also a gardener and seedsman. In 1955 the derelict inn was demolished to make way for a new housing estate.

Hendon Gardens, Gray Road   **Victoria Gardens, China Street**

Like the Strawberry Cottage, the Hendon Gardens and Victoria Gardens took their names from the gardens that stood on their sites. During the last century people from the crowded areas of the East End found a temporary escape in these gardens, where they could buy fruit and picnic. Both these public houses are still in business today.

Grace Darling, Coronation Street

On 10th September 1897, a group of men were drinking in the Grace Darling when the question of how much a man could drink arose. Thirty-year-old Robert Archibold declared that while serving in the Army in India he "drank many a pint of whisky". One of the men ridiculed this claim and a shilling wager was suggested. Despite the fact the men had been drinking from 10.30 a.m. and it was now 2.30 p.m., a half pint of Irish whisky was ordered, which Archibold drank straight off. He was then taken semi-conscious to his aunt's house where he died.

At the inquest the doctor reported the cause of death as, "an overdraught of neat whisky, which had caused paralysis of the nerve centres of the brain". One of the jurymen observed, "Irish whisky is evidently stronger than that supplied to the soldiers in India".

Two weeks after Archibold's death, Rebecca Potts, landlady of the Grace Darling, was fined £5 and costs for selling liquor to a drunken person. At the Licensing Sessions the following August the renewal of the licence of the Grace Darling was opposed. After the owners reported how the previous convicted tenant had been removed the licence was eventually renewed.

James Chrisp, Victualler

The career of Sunderland victualler James Chrisp must go down as one of the most extraordinary in history.

Born in Northumberland in 1830, Chrisp had came to Sunderland as a butler to glass manufacturer, James Hartley. He started life in the licensing trade at the Atlas Inn, High Street East. He made an instant success of his first pub venture. He later recalled the Atlas had been, "worth a guinea a brick to him".

Other public houses were soon acquired by Chrisp, as well as property in Stockton. In 1885 he became a Councillor for Sunderland, going on to serve on several Council Committees. At this time he appeared to have everything in life; wealth, power and influence.

Things began to go disastrously wrong for Chrisp in 1890. On the 1st March of that year he appeared before Durham Assizes accused of assaulting Thomas Hutton, a homeopathic chemist of Villiers Street. At this time Chrisp owned five pubs in town and these were run by barmen he had installed. In one of these, The Shades, High Street East, the Councillor had an argument with Hutton over service in the bar. Chrisp attacked the complaining customer, breaking his walking stick over his head. The jury found him guilty of ejecting Hutton from The Shades with undue force and he was fined £60 and costs.

While a court appearance did not help a public figure like Chrisp, the case was to have far greater consequences for him. At the Licensing Sessions later in the year, Mr. T.W. Backhouse of the temperance movement, made a blistering attack on Chrisp, declaring he was not a fit and proper person to be licensed. Although Chrisp owned other pubs, Backhouse directed his attack on The Shades. Apart from the owner's personal bad character Backhouse said the premises had been conducted in a disorderly

James Chrisp

manner and were unfit for an inn. The Magistrates agreed and withdrew the licence.

The Shades appeared to have a jinx on it for Chrisp. In 1889 he had bought the pub for £3,000 and then spent a further £3,000 on refurbishment. So when the Magistrates removed the licence the following year, Chrisp was £6,000 out of pocket. He naturally tried to recoup his investment by re-applying for the licence in 1891. This was again turned down, as it was in following years.

In 1896 Chrisp made a determined effort to regain The Shades licence. He said he would put in a tenant (which he had also offered in previous attempts) as well as giving up two of his licences. One was near Sunderland Parish Church and the other two doors from St. Patrick's Church. These would then be rebuilt into institutes to serve each church. Despite this offer the licence was refused.

The adverse publicity apparently had an effect on Chrisp's popularity, in 1891 he was defeated in the local elections. The ex-councillor then made another court appearance in October 1893 charged with assaulting labourer, Thomas Reay. The *Sunderland Daily Echo* reported how Chrisp and a young married woman were seen to go into a house together. The woman's husband, along with Reay and others, went into the house and bursting into an upstairs room found the pair 'in a compromising situation'. As Chrisp jumped up Reay grabbed some of his clothes and handed them to one of the other men, saying "Here take these down to the police station". At this point Chrisp grabbed his walking stick and smashed it over Reay's head splitting it open.

Mr. Bell representing Chrisp then set about cross-

S. FAIRMAN & SON,
WINE & SPIRIT MERCHANTS,
No. 13, HOLMESIDE,
AND
"THE SHADES," No. 24, HIGH STREET,
SUNDERLAND.

AGENTS FOR
LACON AND CO.'S YARMOUTH ALES; BASS AND CO.'S BURTON, STRONG, AND INDIA PALE ALES.
SOLE AGENTS FOR
KINAHAN'S CELEBRATED LL. WHISKEY.
(PRIZE MEDAL, DUBLIN EXHIBITION, 1865)
And Château de Condé Champagne.

An advert for Charlie John Fairman's Shades. On 28th September 1887, the pub was ravaged by fire. Two years later Chrisp bought the bar for £3,000 and spent the same amount on refurbishment, which was to prove money down the drain.

examining Reay. When it was suggested he had been under the influence of alcohol when he entered the room, Reay told the court he had only four or five gills (at this time a gill was half a pint) of beer. Amid the laughter of the court he added, "Do you think fower or five gills wad mak me drunk?".

When the tone of Reay's replies to his line of questioning became more agitated, Bell remarked, "Now, now, Reay; you've been here before and ought to know how to conduct yourself".

Reay responded by pointing to Chrisp and saying, "Aye and so has he".

It was revealed Reay had been before the Bench on forty occasions.

After a brief retirement, the Magistrates found the case proved and fined Chrisp £3 and costs.

After his various court appearances and licence battles Chrisp had a change of fortune. In 1894 he returned to the council and was then re-elected on the next three occasions. He continued to build up his pub empire in Sunderland through to the beginning of the twentieth century.

The Chrisp story came to an end in 1905 with the death of the former butler, councillor and pub owner. The final chapter was written in 1908 with the disposal of his property which included six Sunderland pubs.

J. Chrisp & Son,

WHOLESALE AND FAMILY

Wine and Spirit Merchants,

HAVE AT THEIR STORES

24 HIGH STREET EAST, SUNDERLAND,

AN EXTENSIVE STOCK OF WELL MATURED WHISKIES AND WINES.

Scotch and Irish Whiskies, Gin and Pure Jamaica Rum from 2/3 per bottle. Mountain Dew, 3/-. "O. V. G.," Dunvilles' Old Irish, 18/- per gallon, 3/6 per bottle.

SPECIALITY—Blend of Fine Old Scotch Whisky, 16/- per gallon.
Port and Sherry Wines from 2/- per bottle.
Special Old Brandy, 5/6 per bottle.

FINEST BRANDS OF CHAMPAGNE.

The Firm have stocked the above and other Special Choice Stock at their following Houses :

SUNDERLAND :

Dog and Pheasant Hotel, Coronation Street ; Butchers' Arms Hotel, Coronation Street; Bath Hotel, Moor Street ; New Shades Hotel, Hendon Road ; Neptune Hotel, East Woodbine Street ; Golden Lion Hotel, High Street East ; and Sun Inn, High Street, Southwick.

STOCKTON-ON-TEES :

Lambton Castle Hotel, High Street ; William the IV., High Street ; Brown Jug Hotel, Norton Road ; and Regent Hotel, Regent Street.

Price Lists on Application. Large or small orders promptly attended to.

OFFICES : 15 NORFOLK STREET, SUNDERLAND.

National Telephone, Sunderland, No. 787.   Stockton, No. 101.

Ask for CHRISPS' BEEF AND MALT WINE, 2/- and 3/6 per bottle.

An advert from the 1902 Sunderland Year Book listing Chrisp's considerable pub business in Sunderland and Stockton.

The New Shades in Hendon Road, which Chrisp acquired after failing to get a licence for the old Shades in High Street East.

Caledonia Hotel, Lambton Street

This was a family run beerhouse for over a century, ending only in 1978 with the retirement of Tony Thubron and wife Brenda *(above left)*. The couple had ran the pub for 27 years, during which time one of the major memories was of the Joblings Department Store fire in the 1950s. The Caledonia opened, at the request of the police, to house evacuees from the blaze. It then had to close for a week because a nearby chimney was in danger of collapse. In the days when most pub's last orders were at 10.30 p.m., The Caledonia did not serve beer after 10.00 p.m. The pub did not sell spirits until March 1979, having a licence to sell ales, wine and cider only. The Caledonia is now known as The Cally *(above right)*.

Park Inn, Olive Street

In 1902 the Park Inn, after being refurbished at 'considerable expense', was sold at auction for £3,475. The Park Inn today *(above)*.

Theatre Tavern, Lambton Street

This pub took its name from the neighbouring Lyceum Theatre both opening in the 1850s. The Tavern was known to locals as Polly's and this became its official name in the 1980s. Today the pub is known as Coopers' Bar *(above)*.

Opened in 1855, shortly after the nearby Lyceum, the Theatre Royal *(above)* brought business to the surrounding pubs, like the Garrick's Head *(right of picture)*. The names of famous actors and playwrights became popular pub names. At this time there were two Shakespeare Taverns in Sunderland.

Garrick's Head Inn, Bedford Street
After the Theatre Royal was built the Garrick's Head opened to cater for theatre goers. It was named after the famous eighteenth century actor David Garrick. At the time there was already a Kean's Head in Spring Garden Lane, named after the tragic actor, Edmund Kean. In the 1980s the pub was completely refurbished and renamed Pharaoh's. This was a short-lived venture and the pub now goes under the name Mr. Smiths.

CAFE DE L'EUROPE,

5, BEDFORD ST.,

ADJOINING THE THEATRE ROYAL,

SUNDERLAND.

THE MOST

Magnificently fitted up Bars

AND

BILLIARD SALOONS

IN THE NORTH OF ENGLAND.

TWO PUBLIC & ONE RRIVATE TABLE.

JAMES HUDSPITH,
MANAGER.

Cafe de l'Europe, Bedford Street
This unusually named hotel adjoins the old Theatre Royal. It was built at the end of 1860s at a cost of three to four thousand pounds for Arthur Winter. Winter was a German and foreigners in general and his countrymen in particular frequented the establishment. *Above left:* An advert from the 1881-82 *Ward's Directory*. In the 1890s the premises become a temperance hotel and later a lodging house. This establishment was not alone in having a Continental name, in the 1850s there was a Cafe du Commerce in High Street East. Today, the Cafe de l'Europe is now part of the Blue Monkey nightclub *(above right)*.

EMPRESS HOTEL,

UNION STREET, SUNDERLAND,

FIRST-CLASS FAMILY AND COMMERCIAL HOTEL.

Half a minute's walk from the Station.

Cuisine and Wines Unsurpassed. Luncheons daily from 12 to 3 o'clock

BANQUETS CATERED FOR.

SITTING ACCOMMODATION FOR OVER 100.

Tariff on application to Miss SPENCER, Manageress. Telephone No. 83.

Proprietors: JAMES DEUCHAR, LIMITED.
Wine and Spirit Merchants.

Empress Hotel, Union Street
The Empress Hotel (*top*) lay a short distance from the Central Railway Station. *Above:* An advert for the Empress from the early part of the century. During the Second World War it was hit in an air raid and had to be demolished. After the war the bomb site was used by barrow boys (*right*). Although plans were made to rebuild the Empress it never went ahead.

Argo Frigate, West Wear Street
This pub stood near the old Echo Office (now Edward Thompsons). In 1827 the landlord of the Argo Frigate at Ferry Landing was James Weatherburn. In 1971 it closed and shortly afterwards was demolished.

Turf Hotel, West Wear Street
This was another pub that benefited from visitors to the Royal, although it predated the theatre. After having been open for well over a century the Turf closed on 27th March 1960. Florrie Cairns was the last manageress, she had taken over from her father Mark Dixon, who had been manager for 27 years until breaking his hip the previous year. *Above:* Mark Dixon and daughter Florrie.

Mowbray Park Hotel, Toward Road
Originally these premises started life as a thatched cottage called the Gardener's Tavern. In August 1842, after major rebuilding William Alderson opened the Mowbray Arms to the public. This coaching inn had its own billiard table and was stocked with the finest quality wine, spirits, ales and porter. In the 1890s after further reconstruction had been carried out it was renamed the Palatine Hotel. During the 1920s the Palatine underwent major renovation. Tens of thousands of pounds were spent inside and outside the building before opening on 1st March 1927. The completion of another refurbishment in 1971 again signalled a name change, reverting back to the Mowbray Hotel.

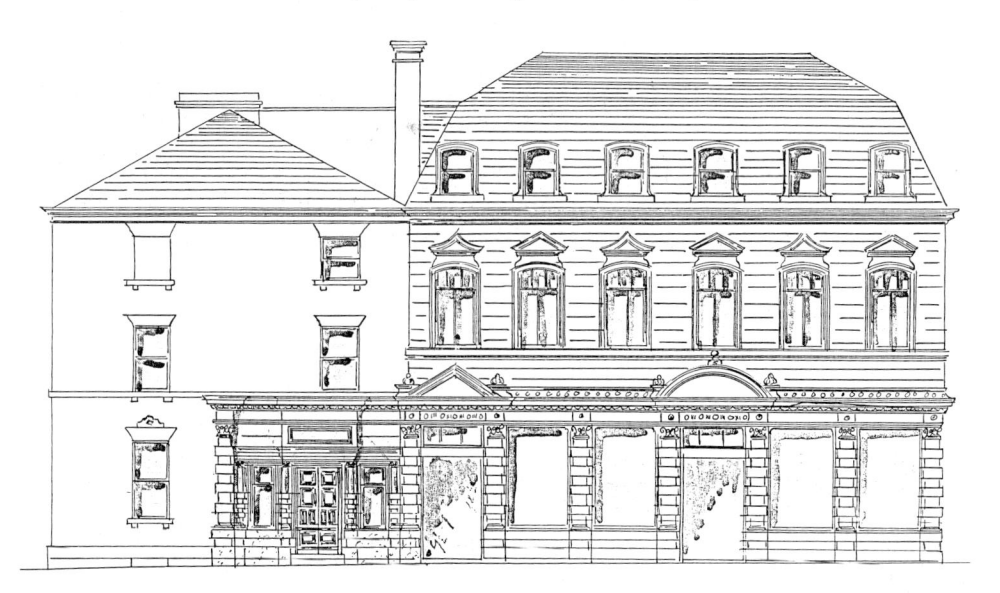

Top and left: Building plans for changes to the Mowbray Hotel in 1894.

Below: The Mowbray earlier this century and today.

The Vestry, Fawcett Street
Originally, this Victorian building was the residence of Sir James Laing, who later converted it into Walton's Hotel. There was one major problem with the location of the hotel: it was opposite the old Town Hall (*above right*) and at night the chimes of the clock kept guests awake. An offer from the hotel's owners to instal equipment to deaden the chimes at night was rejected by the Council. The only alternative was to close the hotel and open it as a bar. Although, this was known by one and all as the Vestry, for most of its life it did not officially have a name. It was licensed as Laing & Company's Bar, 23 Fawcett Street. In 1965 when a 'Vestry sign' was put up, it was the first time its popular name was recognised by the management. The Vestry also had a few other odd quirks. In 1963 it opened on a Sunday for the first time since before the First World War, having just applied for a seven day licence. At this time women were barred from the Vestry and it was to be one of the last Sunderland pubs to admit women. The Vestry is now known as Christies/Fifth Avenue (*above left*).

The Albion, Stockton Road
This pub takes its name from its location in old Albion Place. In December 1983 the Albion reopened after major refurbishment under the new name of Chaplins.

Continental Hotel, St. Thomas Street
The Continental started life at the end of the last century as the Baltic Restaurant and public house. On 14th March 1943 the building that housed the Continental was hit in an air raid, burying this basement bar in rubble (*above left*). (This was the same air raid that hit the Empress Hotel and destroyed St. Thomas Church.) After the war this was eventually rebuilt and on 1st August 1958 the new Continental Hotel was opened (*below*). This differed radically from its predecessor, being a large three storey building. *Above right:* Barmaids at the Continental in the 1960s. In recent years the building has again undergone reconstruction, with only the upstairs remaining as a pub, now called Gillespies.

The Bells, Bridge Street
In the 1880s the Bells (*right*) was owned by James Henderson and later taken over by his sons. One of these, James Potts Henderson, was the first chairman of Sunderland AFC. *Above:* A stained glass window from The Bells depicting Sir Walter Raleigh laying down his cloak for Queen Elizabeth I. When the Bells closed the licence was to 'remain in suspense' until a new pub was built. The Bells was demolished in 1962 but a new pub was never built.

Queen's Hotel, Fawcett Street
Opened in the 1850s, the Queen's established itself as one of the town's top hotels. In 1892 the hotel hosted the Football League's Annual meeting, at which Sunderland received the championship trophy they had won for the first time.

Grand Hotel, Bridge Street
This large five storey building was one of the most famous hotels in Sunderland. Opened in the 1880s, the fifty room hotel finally closed in 1969.

Three Crowns Hotel, High Street West
Above: The old Three Crowns Hotel (with wagon in front) around 1870. This was rebuilt in 1876, becoming one of the busiest and most popular pubs in Sunderland. *Above right:* An advert for the Three Crowns from *Ward's Directory* 1889-90. Landlord, Mr. Moralee remembered how during the war years the Three Crowns was packed every night with sailors from all over the world. "I have had Americans in here who said they first heard of the Three Crowns in Jack Dempsey's bar in New York", he recalled. In September 1959 the pub closed, although, the building still stands. The original glazed tile facade can still be seen today *(below right)*.

The Three Crowns shortly before its closure.

The remains of the Three Crowns today.

Walworth Castle, Walworth Street
The name of this pub derived from Walworth Castle near Darlington. Early in the last century George Harrison inherited land near Crowtree Road. His son bought Walworth Castle and in turn named pub and street after it (*above left and top right*). In 1852 George Boyce was the landlord of the Walworth Castle and on 5th March of that year he appeared before the magistrates. The charge was keeping his house open for drink at 12.20 a.m. the previous day. As it was his first offence he escaped with a caution and was discharged with costs. *Above right:* An advert for the pub early this century. The Walworth Castle was demolished in the late 1960s to make way for the new market square. The naming of Walworth Way being the only link with the past.

Ivy House, Worcester Terrace
The old ivy-clad Ivy House (*left*) dated from the last century. *Above:* The rebuilt Ivy House, today it is popular with students from the nearby university.

The Neptune, Dunning Street
In 1844 the landlord of the Neptune (*above*) was James Gray. It was known to locals as the 'Number Nine' (its number in the street). The embarrassing situation of having a pub from a rival brewery in the middle of the Vaux complex was resolved in 1974. Vaux exchanged the Clousden Hill public house at Forest Hall, Newcastle for the Whitbread-owned Neptune. The start of a new era for the pub was accompanied by a name change to the Brewery Tap (*above right*).

The Licensing session on 4th June 1931 decided three pubs were to be closed down. These were the Cottage Tavern, Hopper Street; Neptune Hotel, East Woodbine Street and the Newcastle Arms, Ropery Lane. The owners of the Neptune Hotel told the magistrates they were willing to spend £3,500 on rebuilding the pub if the licence was renewed. The magistrates rejected this proposal and referred all three pubs for compensation.

Oak Bar, South Street
On 14th March 1943, in the same air raid that wrecked the Empress Hotel and Continental, William Jackson from the Oak Bar was taken to hospital with serious injuries. This pub was popular with policemen from the nearby Gill Bridge Station. In 1970 the Oak Bar closed for the last time.

Commercial Vaults, Green Street
Right: This pub was known as the 'Long Bar' because it had the longest counter in town. The Long Bar was another casualty of town centre redevelopment.

Sons of the Wear, Queen Street
Above: In 1834 this pub was run by John Crick. The origin of its name may have come from a poem of that name published in 1781. Thomas Clarke's 'Sons of the Wear' included the lines:

> Ye Social few with hearts ever true,
> Unshaken by gold or by fear,
> Who meet with a view every grief to subdue,
> And regale over Martin's * good cheer,
> Be happy and free, each glass fill with glee,
> Success to the Sons of the Wear,

* James Martin was landlord of the Golden Lion in High Street East.

White Hart, Queen Street
Right: The Landlord of the White Hart in 1834 was one Lancelot Herring. It went on to become one of the town centre's most popular pubs. In the 1960s plans were drawn up for a new ring road and the White Hart had to go. However, no one told the landlord his pub was to be demolished, he was informed by a customer who had read it in the *Sunderland Echo*.

COLLAPSE OF A BUILDING IN BRIDGE-STREET.

EXCITING SCENES.

Bridge End Vaults, Bridge Street
On the evening of 23rd May 1890 the Bridge End Vaults collapsed without warning. The pub had been undergoing major renovation when the building suddenly fell down, burying workmen under the rubble. The last of the men was recovered after being entombed for two hours. Fortunately, none had serious injuries. The following day the *Sunderland Daily Echo* reported on the scene of devastation (*left*).

The Bridge End Vaults was rebuilt and survived until October 1967, when it closed to make way for road development.

Right: The landlady for the last dozen years of its life had been Mrs. Ann Thompson.

Below: The Bridge End Vaults shortly before its demolition.

Blandford House, Blandford Street
The old Blandford House in the 1930s (*above*). The Blandford in the 1950s (*left*). Today, it stands in a traffic free zone allowing the pub to put tables in the street and serve drink 'European style'.

DICK EDDY,

"BROUGHAM ARMS,"

Brougham Street

(Near the South End of Central Station)

Ales, Wines, & Spirits,

OF THE FINEST QUALITY.

Brougham Arms, Brougham Street
Right: This nineteenth century pub had a music room upstairs where people played the piano or accordion and then passed round a hat for a few coppers. *Above right:* An advert from the 1910 *Sunderland Year Book*. In 1963 it was closed and demolished to make way for the new town centre development. *Above:* Elsie Peterson was the last landlady of the Brougham Arms. The bus station now stands on Brougham Street.

Masons' Arms, Dunning Street
In the days when off course betting was illegal, the Masons' Arms was continually associated with bookmaking. At the 1906 Licensing Sessions, the police opposed the pub's license renewal on the grounds it was a 'hotbed of bookmaking'. They recalled how the previous tenant had been found guilty of keeping premises as a betting house. The pub was popular with bookies who plied their trade in the surrounding streets. During the Second World War the Masons' Arms was lucky to survive, as buildings on the opposite side of the street were destroyed by landmines in an air raid. In October 1967 the Masons' Arms was finally reduced to rubble to make way for the new ring road.

Bricklayers' Arms, Central Railway Station
This pub lay at the north end of the old Central Railway Station. When the station was redeveloped for the 1966 World Cup the pub was forced to close. Littlewoods department store now stands on the site.

Crown and Thistle, High Street West
Left: In 1881 this pub had some unexpected visitors. The Waverly Hotel, which stood opposite, collapsed with five customers inside. When these were dug out they were carried to the Crown and Thistle to recover. In the early 1960s the pub was served with a compulsory purchase order and demolished.

Vaux Brewery

When Cuthbert Vaux went into partnership with W. Story around 1806 it was the beginning of what was to be one of Sunderland's most successful and longest surviving businesses.

By 1837 the partnership had been dissolved and C. Vaux & Co. was formed at a brewery on the corner of Cumberland Street and Matlock Street. By 1844 the company had expanded and bought a brewery in Union Street where business continued until 1875. In that year the North Eastern Railway Company bought the site for the new Central Station. Vaux then moved to Castle Street and Gill Bridge Avenue where they remain to this day. Three years after the business passed into the hands of his sons, John Story Vaux and Colonel Edwin Vaux. After the death of John Story in 1887, his sons Major Cuthbert Vaux and Colonel Ernest Vaux joined their uncle Edwin in the company.

A large fleet of horse drays carried the brewery's wares to the pubs around Wearside. While steam traction engines and later petrol driven lorries were introduced, horses were never completely replaced. Percheron horses were imported from France and in more recent years

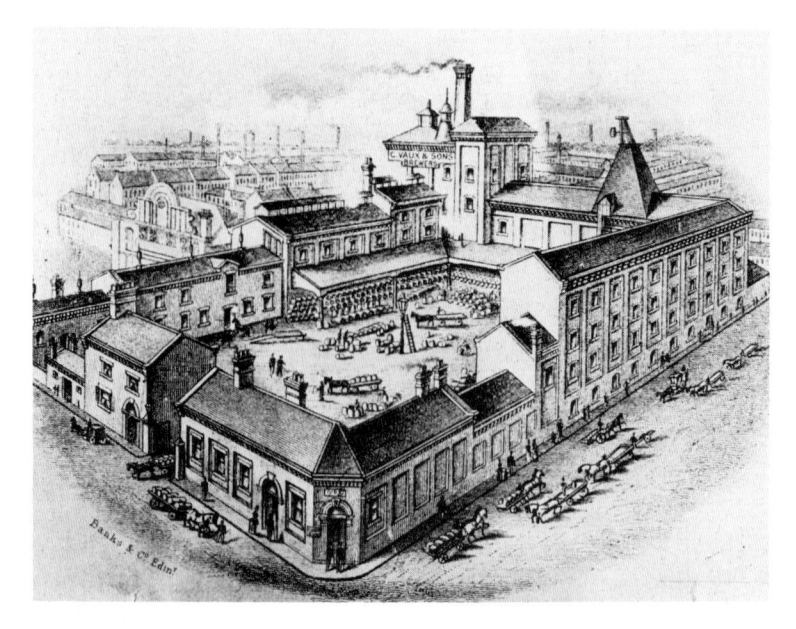

Vaux Brewery in 1875.

Vaux drays at the turn of the century. The horseman (right foreground) holding the reins was called Ellie Smith. He was able to lift full barrels onto his dray by himself. The junk yard (front right) is now Vaux's main office block.

A steam engine dray alongside horse drays around the time of the First World War.

Gelderlanders from Holland. The large grey Percheron are still an impressive sight on the streets of Sunderland today. Horses have proved cost effective when deliveries are less than five miles from the Brewery. Savings are made on not having to pay vehicle tax, horse feed replacing petrol and the only maintenance are vet fees and horse shoes. The initial outlay is much less than that for lorries and the working life of a horse of ten years compares favourably with motor transport.

In the early part of the last century Vaux was just one among dozens of breweries in Sunderland. Others included: Bramwell's Wear Brewery, Horn and Scott's, Mark Quay and Fenwick's (later Flowers). The Subscription Brewery was unusual because the dividends to shareholders were paid in ale and beer.

Frank Nicholson joined the company in 1898, becoming Manager and Secretary. He later married Cuthbert Vaux's sister Amy. In 1914 he became a director of the company and in 1919 Managing Director.

Vaux's expansion centred on establishing bottling plants in places like Middlesbrough, Leeds and Glasgow. After the First World War Vaux acquired a number of small breweries, which increased their holdings in pubs as well as brewing capacity. One of these breweries was Lorimer and Clark which brought Scotch beer to Wearside (Lorimers Scotch is still sold today).

In 1927 Vaux amalgamated with former rivals North Eastern Breweries Ltd. The new company was called Associated Breweries, which became Vaux and Associated Breweries Ltd. and since 1973 Vaux Breweries Ltd.

Almost 190 years after they first began to brew on Wearside, Vaux are still in business. Today, the company's interests include brewing, public houses, wine and spirits sales and the Swallow hotel chain.

Part of the Vaux lorry fleet between the wars. Petrol engine transport replaced steam engines but has still not fully replaced horse drays even today.

Black Bull, High Street West

The Black Bull is mentioned in an advert in 1772, at which time it was a cottage inn serving Bishopwearmouth. In the middle of the last century it was rebuilt with pride of place going to the large figure of a black bull. This can be seen in an advert from the beginning of the century (*above right*). In the 1980s after a major renovation the old pub was renamed Scott's (*above left*).

Painted Wagon, Holmeside

This was an example of a modern pub that had a short lived career. It is remembered for an infamous pitched battle in 1978, which took place in the pub and nearby car park. This left a student on a life support machine, he survived but remains brain damaged in Ryhope Hospital to this day. The Painted Wagon closed in the 1980s.

Londonderry Hotel, High Street West
On the site of the present day Londonderry stood the Peacock Inn. In the eighteenth century this was Bishopwearmouth's principal coaching inn. In 1772 an advert appeared for Robert Moor of Durham which stated "he was prepared to collect and bleach linen and yarn, a receiving place for these goods being Mrs. Wilson, The Peacock, High Street". By 1834 the inn was known as the Londonderry Arms. *Above*: The old Londonderry during the last century. In 1901 this was replaced by the present building (*right*).

Dun Cow, Dun Cow Street
When the norm was for pubs to often take their name from streets in which they stood, the Dun Cow gave its name to the street. The old Dun Cow (*above left*) first appeared in Directories in 1834 when Chapman Braithwaite was the landlord. In 1901 the present Dun Cow was completely rebuilt in baroque style (*above right*).

OXO Flavoured CRISTO CRISPS

Manufactured by W. Methwich Ltd.

THE HOST WHO CATERS FOR HIS PUBLIC
SELLS OXO CRISPS
THE GREATEST OF ALL GOOD CRISPS
... HE CAN'T AFFORD TO BE WITHOUT THEM

GIRVAN NICHOLL & Son
187 ROKER AVENUE, SUNDERLAND. Tel. 56621
TRADE SUPPLIED

X·L POTATO CRISPS X·L
NO GREASY GLASSES WITH X·L CRISPS
THEY ARE EXTRA FINE DRIED

MADE SPECIALLY FOR THE LICENSED TRADE — **3D.** — PACKED IN HYGIENIC NON-RETURNABLE CARTONS

THE CRISPS CUSTOMERS COME BACK FOR

3D. GIRVAN NICHOLL & SON,
187 ROKER AVENUE,
SUNDERLAND
Telephone 56621
(MAIN NORTHERN AGENTS) **3D.**

Above and left: 1950s adverts from local crisp manufacturers for the ever popular pub snack. In the not too distant past, people were not always certain about what they were purchasing in pubs. On 22nd April 1949, a woman was found guilty at South Shields Magistrates of "manufacturing for sale pies and sandwiches containing horse flesh." When police found her in possession of 40 to 50 'horse' pies and enquired about their destination, she replied, "they will be sold round the pubs in Sunderland."

Queen's Head, Low Row

Above: The Queen's Head was one of the oldest pubs in Bishopwearmouth until its closure in the 1960s. In 1820 Sarah Sewell was its landlady. Thirteen years later the Queen's Head was put up for sale *(right)*.

To be Sold
BY AUCTION,
On Tuesday, the 3rd of September, 1833,
At Seven o'Clock in the Evening,
AT THE QUEEN'S HEAD INN,
LOW ROW, BISHOPWEARMOUTH,

Mr. Hartforth, Auctioneer,

All that the said old-established and most desirable

PUBLIC HOUSE,
Known by the Name of the Queen's Head Inn,

Now occupied by Mr. John Cowell, most advantageously situated for trade in the Low Row, Bishopwearmouth, comprising a convenient and spacious DWELLING HOUSE, containing 10 good Fire-Rooms, Cellars, &c. with a spacious YARD behind the same, containing in length 29 Yards, and in breadth 11 Yards; together with a large

NEW BUILDING

Attached thereto, suitable either for a STABLE or COW BYER. Also, another

EXTENSIVE YARD,

Immediately adjoining the Premises on the South, containing 44 Yards in length, and about 8 Yards wide; together with a convenient

Dwelling House

Therein, occupied by Anthony Mawson;

THREE EXCELLENT STABLES,

Calculated to accommodate 8 Horses, and with all other necessary conveniences. There is a good approach to the Yards and Stables, both from the back and front of the Premises.

The Premises are Copyhold of Inheritance, subject only to an Out-rent of Sixpence Halfpenny annually. This Property being in the immediate entrance of the populous Town of Bishopwearmouth from the great South Roads, having been carried on as an Inn for a great number of Years, and from the great accommodation it possesses, presents a desirable situation for carrying on an extensive and lucrative Business.

For further Particulars apply to the Auctioneer; or to Mr. J. J. Wright, Solicitor, Sunderland; or Mr. Brignal, Solicitor, Durham.

Sunderland, 15th August, 1833.

SUNDERLAND: PRINTED BY REED AND SON.

Hat and Feather Vaults, Low Row   **Imperial Vaults, Lambton Street**

Early this century the Imperial Vaults and the Hat and Feather Vaults were both owned by Arthur Green. At this time the Imperial was known as 'Greens'. While the Imperial is still in business today it is no longer known as Greens. The Hat and Feather Vaults, however, is now officially called 'The Greens'.

Above: The original Hat and Feather Hotel.

Charles Green & Co.,
RETAILERS OF
Foreign Wines and Spirits.

ALE, PORTER & CIGAR MERCHANTS.

HAT AND FEATHER VAULTS
LOW ROW.

TELEPHONE, 1006.

Above: An advert for Charles Green's Hat and Feather Vaults.

Central Hotel, Bridge Street
The Central has survived when its near neighbours: The Grand, Three Crowns, Bridge End Vaults, Commercial Vaults and The Bells have all long since disappeared. On 31st May 1910, The Central was offered for sale at the Palatine Hotel. After bidding started at £12,000 it had reached £17,400 when it was declared sold. However, the purchaser did not pay the deposit and the auctioneer offered the property to the bidder who had offered £17,300. When the second highest bidder declined this offer the sale began again. This time W.B. Reid and Co. of Newcastle bought The Central at the knocked down price of £16,400.

Burton House Hotel, Borough Road
In 1894 there was no less than seven pubs in Sunderland named Burton House. The Burton House in Borough Road is the only one to have survived. In March 1983, landlord, Sammy Doran offered an alternative to the usual brews: milk. This was not a new drink to pubs, however, at the turn of the century milk had been popular, often taken with whisky.

Coach and Horses, High Street West
This pub dated from at least the early part of the nineteenth century, in 1820 William Blacket was landlord. Later in the century it was rebuilt. *Right:* The Coach and Horses shortly before its closure in 1959.

George and Dragon, High Street West

This was originally an old inn serving Bishopwearmouth village. In 1820 John Ranson was landlord of this popular central public house. In 1891 the Palace Theatre was built next door, and during this decade under the ownership of Mr. Waddle, major improvements to the George and Dragon were made. This included a billiard saloon with five tables under the care of Mr. Benneworth, a well known player.

Right: An advert for Waddle's George and Dragon in 1902.

THE
GEORGE & DRAGON
HIGH STREET WEST,
Has the **FINEST**
BILLIARD ROOM IN THE NORTH OF ENGLAND
5 NEW TABLES. Electric Light Throughout.
WADDLE'S SPECIAL, A TREAT.

Below: Further renovation was carried out this century included a new frontage. The Crowtree Leisure Centre now stands on the site of the George and Dragon.

Rose and Crown, High Street West

In his *History of Sunderland*, W.C. Mitchell claims the Rose and Crown was built in 1615. It was certainly a pub in 1790. On New Years's night 1884, a seaman called Collie and his friends were refused service in the Rose and Crown because they were the worse for drink. Collie then gathered all the glasses on the counter into his arms and began to throw them at the landlord, Mr. Wingate. Two found their target, striking Wingate on the head, resulting in great loss of blood. After being charged with grievous bodily harm, Collie was found guilty and given a month's imprisonment. *Above*: The old Rose and Crown, with a shop on the corner separating two entrances. *Above right*: An advert from 1902 *Sunderland Year Book*. *Below*: The modernised building, with shop removed. In 1969 The Rose and Crown and the adjoining Cobden Exchange were demolished to make way for the inner ring road.

Lambton Arms, Crowtree Road
Like its neighbour the Londonderry, it too had been named after a local landowning family. In 1844 Simpson Hodgson was landlord at the Lambton Arms. The pub was lucky to survive a raid during the last war. On 16th May 1943 incendiary bombs destroyed the King's Theatre which stood next door. *Left:* The Lambton Arms with the derelict cinema on the left (which was finally demolished in 1954). The Lambton Arms itself was to meet its end in the town centre redevelopment of the late 1960s and early 1970s.

Royal Tent, High Street West
This old pub was in a row of property in front of St. Michael's Church, Bishopwearmouth. In the early part of the last century Jane Allison was landlady at the Royal Tent. In the 1930s it was demolished to allow the road in front to be widened.

Above: Three pubs in a row in Crowtree Road: The Crowtree Inn, Three Tuns and Red Lion. All three pubs dated from the nineteenth century or earlier. The **Crowtree Inn** was a beerhouse and was known in the 1890s as the Crow Tavern. The **Three Tuns** had as its landlord in 1827 Gilbert Hodgson. Alexander Baharie claimed the **Red Lion** was built in 1630 but this is questioned by some historians. The Leisure Centre now stands on the site of all three pubs.

Boilermakers' Arms, High Street West

James Corder records how the licence for this pub had been transferred from the Friendly Tavern which had stood in Horsley's Fold in the last century. After this had been rebuilt to the street line it became the Boilermakers' Arms. Having fallen into disuse, the Council approved its conversion to a 'live Victorian Public House Museum' in 1974. Two years later, Council Leader Len Harper opened the refurbished pub under the name 'Old Twenty Nine' (its number in the street). However, its new career was to be short lived and in the 1980s it was demolished.

The Tea Shop, High Street West

Although officially called the Scotch House this pub was known to locals as the 'Tea Shop'. This was because at one time tea was sold from a large canister from behind the bar. An unusual feature of this one room bar was that the seats and tables were made from oak barrels. These had come from a Devon port where they had been used to transport water and provisions out to 'Man of War' ships. In September 1970 The Tea Shop broke a 108-year-old tradition by allowing women in for the first time. The pub closed its doors for the last time in the 1980s. *Above:* Barmen in the Tea Shop in the 1960s.

The Royalty, Chester Road

The Royalty is known to regulars as The Glebe. This is because the nineteenth century Glebe Hotel stood on the site prior to The Royalty. In July 1937 at the Licensing Sessions the owners sought to demolish and rebuild the pub, doubling the size of the drinking area. As the Corporation also wanted to widen Chester Road the scheme got the go ahead. The original name had derived from ancient times when the glebe was church owned land, most of which was farmed. The site where the pub was later to stand, at the end of the eighteenth century, was at the edge of 130 acres of glebe land which ran up to High Barnes

North Moor, Durham Road

The North Moor was nicknamed the Yellow Bird Shop. It got its name from a bird shop which stood in Silksworth Row before the war. The building was painted a vivid yellow like the pub. Since the 1970s the North Moor has been known as the Double Maxim. In comparison with other areas of Sunderland the pubs in this neighbourhood are few and far between. During this century, as housing estates expanded westward, the Licensing Authorities were able to control the number of new pubs.

On the 6th March, 1936, Licensing Justices gave the go ahead for the building of three new hotels in the town by granting provisional licences. These were for the Barnes Hotel, Pallion Inn and Seaburn Hotel.

Pallion Inn, St. Luke's Terrace
At the 1936 Licensing Session, North Eastern Breweries successfully applied for the transfer of the Dog and Pheasant, Coronation Street to the planned Pallion which would cost an estimated £5,000 to build. The Brewery also surrendered the licences of the Pallion Inn, Lister Street, the Skiff Inn, Slater Street, Deptford and an off-licence. The Chief Constable said the police had no objection to this and added "we are pleased to see the last of the Dog and Pheasant". *Above left:* The Pallion Inn during the 1950s and today *(above right).*

Barnes Hotel, Durham Road
Left: This hotel was built on an island site and was due to cost £12,000. The licence from the Oddfellows' Arms, Barclay Street was transferred for this new hotel. The owners proposed the surrender of three other pubs: The Neptune, Pilgrim Street Southwick, the Banks of the Wear, Ayre's Quay and the Foresters' Arms, Albert Street.

Seaburn Hotel, Whitburn Road
Right: This was the most expensive project costing £20,000 and took only fourteen weeks to complete. A decorative 'lighthouse' stood on the roof but was never used as it could be a danger to shipping. In recent years the Seaburn has been completely refurbished and now goes under the name the Swallow Hotel.

Temperance

The modern temperance movement started with the Quakers in America in the 1770s. While they ultimately achieved their goal of prohibition (1920-1933) there was never the same success in this country. In the 1830s a number of temperance societies were founded in cities in the north of England. In 1833 the word teetotaller was first used by a reformed drunkard, Dick Turner.

In nineteenth century Sunderland there were many different temperance organisations, these included: British Women's Temperance Association, Sons of Temperance, Band of Hope, Temperance Society, Church of England Temperance Society and The North of England Temperance Society.

The temperance movement was always well represented at the Licensing Sessions, opposing new licences and renewals whenever the opportunity arose. Guides were published giving advice on how best to exert influence at the Licensing Sessions. One popular title was *How to Shut Up a Public House*. The movement also had some influential leaders, notably T.W. Backhouse. He had the wealth to be able to employ Queen's Councils on behalf of the temperance cause at Licensing Sessions. As in the famous Chrisp case (page 34).

As well as trying to reduce the number of public houses in town, the temperance movement also used

T.W. Backhouse

A High Street East Wesleyan Band of Hope pledge from the last century.

education, especially amongst the young. The Band of Hope had been formed in 1847 and aimed at children under 16. It was based on the pledge, "I do agree that I will not use intoxicating liquor as a beverage". Sunderland Band of Hope was established in 1881 and went into schools to lecture children, organising outings and held an annual demonstration and party. On 28th July 1894 thousands of children from the 33 Band of Hope branches marched from Holmeside via Stockton Road to Lee's Field at Ryhope. The procession was led by banners and the Orphan Asylum band followed by the 'little waterdrinkers' with their blue ribbons stretching back for a mile. When they finally reached the field, games were organised and tea, bread and cakes served.

By 1897 the Band of Hope had a nationwide membership of 3,200,000 children. Although membership declined in the twentieth century the zeal of their leaders had not. In May 1948, the Durham County Band of Hope held its annual conference in Sunderland. Organiser, Edward Child attacked brewers' advertising campaigns as being aimed at children. He cited pubs providing play grounds for youngsters and posters showing nursery rhyme characters drinking beer as evidence of this. He also tried to put the £685 million spent on drink annually in perspective. At the time when there was still food rationing, he said, "If people did not drink beer, Britain would effect a saving sufficient to provide this country with four thousand million eggs and all the bacon we wanted".

```
SMITH'S TEMPERANCE HOTEL,
       74 High Street West,
(Corner of Cumberland Street),  SUNDERLAND.

CLOSE TO STATION, THEATRES AND HALLS.

A POPULAR HOTEL FOR COMMERCIAL GENTLEMEN.
       EVERY COMFORT AND ATTENTION.
```

An advert for one of a number of temperance hotels in Sunderland at the turn of the century.

On 14th August 1877 a public house that did not sell alcohol was opened in Wellington Lane, Ayres Quay. The object was to attract shipyard and foundry workers away from the regular pubs. The 'Deptford British Workman' offered cheap food, meat and potatoes with bread cost only 6d. As well as a dining room there was also a reading room and smoking room. The pub without beer was a success, workmen paid a subscription of a halfpenny a week which helped keep prices down. In January of the following year St. John's British Workman opened in the East End of town.

Another alternative to the regular public house came in 1881 with the founding of the Sunderland Coffee Tavern (Ltd.). Its aim was to open taverns like ordinary pubs except no intoxicating liquor would be sold. *Above*: High Street West Coffee Tavern (centre of picture) around 1890. Within three years there was a total of eight coffee taverns in town, as well as one in Southwick.

Fish Inn, Silksworth Row
Thousands of people pass this former beerhouse every day without knowing it is there. Dating from the last century, the Fish Inn has been closed many years.

Museum Vaults, Silksworth Row
This old beerhouse dates from the last century when it was known as 'The Museum and Curiosity Vaults'. Its landlord in 1871 was Herbert Matthews. A legacy of its beerhouse days was a lack of spirit licence. This was not rectified until 1978 when it became one of the last pubs in Sunderland to be granted a licence to sell spirits.

> While members of the temperance movement tried to persuade drunks to see the error of their ways, at times words were not enough. From 1895 to 1910 St. Luke's in Pallion had a vicar who at times resorted to more forceful means. In *Pallion 1874 to 1954: Church and People in a Shipyard Parish*, C.H.G. Hopkins recalled how Reverend Septimus Porter "had a short and effective way of coping with drunks .... a straight left from the vicar would soon put then to sleep if they were giving trouble".

Ship Isis, Silksworth Row
A few years ago this pub was renamed Livingstones *(right)*, after the nearby Livingstone Road. The Ship Isis dates from the early part of the last century, the present building was built in 1885. Originally the name of the pub was The Ship. The crew of a ship called the Isis were regularly paid off in the Silksworth Row bar. After locals began to call it the Ship Isis it officially changed its name.

Black Swan, Silksworth Row
The Black Swan was located in the Hodgson Building in 1823. The pub also had its own brewery in Hodgson Building, both being taken over by Nicholas Moody in 1853. *Above*: The old Black Swan early this century when John Chipchase was the owner. *Below*: The new Black Swan in the 1950s when it was known as the 'Mucky Duck'. Although no longer a pub the building still stands today.

When licensing restrictions were lifted in 1830, it allowed any householder who had the two guinea fee, to set up a beerhouse. This was reflected in some odd combinations of professions. In 1831 John Alder of Low Street was listed in Directories as a Tailor, Slopseller and Publican. The pub Alder ran was The Angel in Low Street. The Angel closed when it was taken over by Joblings and Tuer in High Street to extend their premises towards Low Street.

Westbury Arms, Westbury Street
John Armstrong was a manager of the Westbury Arms *(above)* in the late 1950s. He was an example of the nomadic nature of the life of a licensee. He started work under his father in Throckley Club before going to work in premises in Newcastle. In 1932 he moved to Sunderland to take over the Jamaica Vaults. He was then manager of The Albion, Dock Street; Southwick Club and Bath Hotel before taking over the Westbury. He was awaiting a move to a new pub, the Hylton Castle Arms, when he died aged 51. The Westbury was demolished in the 1960s and a church now stands on the site.

Caledonian Arms, Trimdon Street
In 1871 the Caledonian Arms had Sarah Matthews as its landlady. In the last century a large proportion of women ran pubs. In contrast the majority of customers were men.

In the last century many inns and beerhouses had unusual names. These included: **Topsy's Happy Home Tavern**, Lombard Street; **Better Luck Still**, Crescent Row; **Belgian Arms**, St. Cuthbert Terrace; **Little Wonder**, Drury Lane; **Hole in the Wall**, Low Street; **Three Indian Kings**, Hodgkin Street; **Friend's Goodwill**, Burleigh Street; **Gasometer**, Grey Street and **Labour in Vain**, Union Lane.

An all-male outing leaving the Caledonian in the 1920s.

Live and Let Live, Gerald Street 
Despite its odd name there was more than one Live and Let Live in Sunderland at one time. As well as this one at the Ballast Hills in Deptford (*right*), there was another in Low Street in the 1940s. In an article in the *Sunderland Echo* of 5th February 1959, Nel Rachford recalled how locals at the Gerald Street pub formed a 'cork club', subscribing each week for a Christmas party. "Each member was given a small cork bearing the initials L.A.L.L. One eventful day the stars must have been operating for those worthy members. The big horse race of the day included among the runners a horse by the name of Lall. On the book of form he had not the remotest chance. Yet every man jack of the L.A.L.L. club put his shirt on him. He skated in at 20 to 1. It was pints all round at the Live and Let Live that night." When the pub closed it was used as a private residence for a number of years. Today, even this has long since gone.

Saltgrass Inn, Hanover Place
The Saltgrass takes its name from the tidal wet land that one time stood on the Deptford riverside. This area had originally been called Southwick, today only the opposite north bank bears this name. In the last century the Saltgrass (*left*) was one of many pubs in Ayre's Quay. *Bottom left:* Today, it is one of the few survivors. In 1944, however, if the licensee at the time had been allowed the Saltgrass would have closed. At the Licensing Sessions, landlord, Ralph Heppell, on behalf of Vaux & Co. applied to have the licence transferred from the Saltgrass Inn to St. Mark's Vicarage in Chester Road. It was then proposed to demolish this and rebuild a hotel on the site after the war and call it The Chesters. The Saltgrass at this time was still doing a 'substantial trade' and was valued at £4,000. The Magistrates rejected the transfer allowing the Saltgrass to survive to this day.

Aylmer Arms, Aylmer Street
This beerhouse was popular after the war with a bookie's 'runner'. He had no legs and got about on a kind of skateboard. On one occasion he was being chased by the police when he took refuge in the Aylmer's passageway. With the police hot on his trail he avoided arrest by hiding in a dustbin.

Rising Sun, Trimdon Street
Being near to Millfield Railway Station gave the Rising Sun a lot of passing trade. Jimmy Gorman, who played in Sunderland's 1937 FA Cup winning team, was for a time landlord of the Rising Sun.

Mountain Daisy, Hylton Road
There was a Mountain Daisy in Hylton Road in 1844 when Ann Harper was landlady. The present building (*left*) dates from 1901. Some of the rooms in the pub have been preserved as they were at the turn of the century. One downstairs room still has its original glazed wall tiles.

The Beehive, Hylton Road
In 1853 John Hope was landlord of the Beehive in Hylton Road. The present building, however, was built in 1881 *(above)*. In the 1960s its name was changed to The Beefeater. Later there was another name change, to Oddies. The present licensees of Oddies are John and Pat Royal.

The recently erected Oddies sign.

Oddies today.

John and Pat Royal.

Sportsman's Arms, Deptford Road
Left: In 1871, Henry Kilburn was the landlord of this beerhouse. It comprised a Bar, Parlour and Taproom on the ground floor and a Club Room upstairs. On 12th June 1893 it was offered for sale but withdrawn after bidding only reached £530.

Pubs and Rowing

In the last century rowing was popular on the Wear and public houses played their part in the sport. A race between the champions of the Wear, Alexander Hogarth of Monkwearmouth and Joseph Cunningham of Southwick was arranged for 30th October 1876. This was to be for a stake of £25 and both men had to make deposits at Mr. Cowell's Minerva Hotel in East Cross Street. The race took place in 24 foot long boats on a course between Crown House Quay and Hylton Chains. Hogarth won by 15 lengths in a time of 15 minutes. The trainer of Hogarth was a Mr. Morgan of the Ship Inn at Silksworth. Cunningham was also a landlord of a public house, he ran the Rower's Arms in Collin Place, Southwick. This was not the only pub name with a rowing theme. The Skiff Inn, Slater Street took its name from a light sculling boat. As well as at Sunderland, racing also took place on the Wear at Durham and on the Tyne. Corder recalls how local favourite Elliott raced Hanlon the Canadian on the Tyne. One avid follower was Potts, owner of the Black Bull in High Street who put money on Elliott to win. After the race he wired home to Sunderland, "Elliott. beaten. Hanlon. grand. man." The Black Bull read this as, "Elliott beaten Hanlon, grand man" and, "bellowing with joy stood free drinks all round". On returning Potts demanded an explanation as to how his communication had been misread, but it was too late the bets and the drinks were long gone.

Black Cow, Ravensworth Street
Left: The Black Cow was a tiny bar with a dartboard over the fire place. Shortly before its demolition in the 1950s a championship deciding dart match took place there. When one of the locals lost the crucial game he threw his darts up the chimney in disgust. When the building was being pulled down he went back and found the three lost darts.

The Lansdowne, Lansdowne Street
Left: The Lansdowne during the 1930s. Dating from the middle of the last century, the Lansdowne recently changed its name to Cooper's Tavern (*above*).

Kings Arms, Hanover Place
This Deptford pub is one of the oldest in Sunderland dating from at least 1834, when Jane Davison was landlady. *Above:* The King's Arms today.

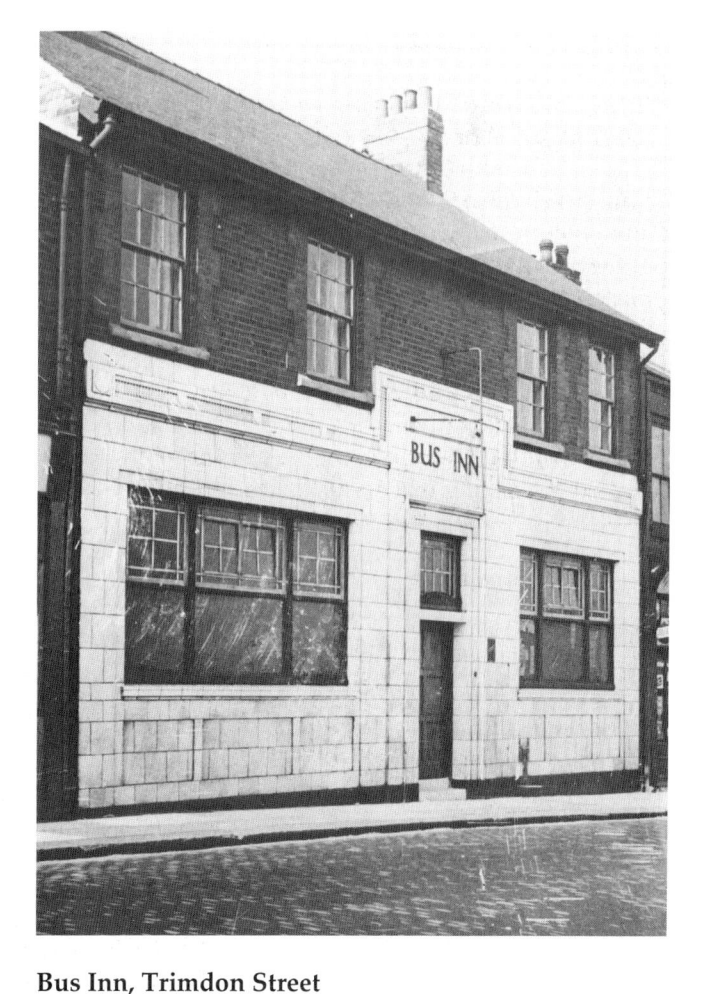

Bus Inn, Trimdon Street
This was one of numerous beerhouses in Trimdon Street which have now all gone. In 1871 the Bus Inn was run by Richard Meek.

Willow Pond, Hylton Road
In 1870s William Sowter ran the Willow Pond, which 120 years later is still going strong (*above*).

Crown and Sceptre, Hylton Road
In 1844 Ann Royal ran the Crown and Sceptre in Millfield. More than 120 years later the Crown and Sceptre was closed and the building demolished.

Temple Bar, South Johnson Street
The Temple Bar disappeared in the post-war slum clearances. Pubs were usually the last to be demolished, often standing by themselves for years.

General Havelock, Trimdon Street
This beerhouse on the corner of Trimdon Street and Glass Street consisted of a Large Bar, Sitting Room and Snug. The pub took its name from Bishopwearmouth-born, General Sir Henry Havelock of Indian Mutiny fame. Another soldier from this campaign, Sir Colin Campbell, also gave his name to a Sunderland pub. This one being in High Street East. The General Havelock lying derelict *(above)*.

Oddfellows' Arms, Trimdon Street
Above: This pub was known to locals as Boucher's after former owners. The pub's most endurable landlords were James and Peggy Carter, who ran the Oddfellows for over forty years. Mrs. Carter celebrated her 100th birthday in April 1993.

The Antelope, Trimdon Street
This nineteenth century pub was put up for sale on 30th May 1910 at the Palatine Hotel. Prior to the sale an advert appeared in the *Sunderland Daily Echo*.

> Lot 6 - The Copyhold Fully-licensed Public-house situate No. 1, TRIMDON STREET WEST, known as the
> **Antelope**
> being at the corner of Trimdon Street West (frontage about 42ft. 6in.) and Enderby Road (frontage about 70ft.), and is favourable situated in a main thoroughfare of the thickly-populated district of Deptford. The Inn comprises large bar, family department and smokeroom on ground floor; five rooms on first floor; large cellar; warehouse and convenience in yard. The site of this house is held subject to the annual payment of £2 5s 4d.

Free Gardeners Arms, Grafton Street
This example of a street corner pub is unusual, in that, the terrace of houses are bungalows.

Railway Tavern, Westbury Street
This was one of many pubs that catered for workers from nearby glass making factories. Because of the hot, hard nature of their work, glass blowers were allowed to drink beer as a concession. On one occasion the boy sent to get the men's beer from the Railway was arrested by the police for buying alcohol under age. When the boy was taken to court the men had a whip round to pay his fine.

Oddfellows Arms, North Ravensworth Street
At one time there was a number of Oddfellows Arms in Sunderland. The name comes from the societies formed in the last century to help its members in time of sickness or distress. This Oddfellows is known to locals as Ted's, after Ted Elliott a former landlord.

Shoulder of Mutton, Ropery Road
In the middle of last century the Shoulder of Mutton was just one of many pubs serving the industrial workers of Deptford. Many of the names of pubs reflected the various manufacturers in the area at the time. There was the Ship Launch, Forge Tavern and Bottlemakers' Arms. Glassmaking was a major employer, Ayre's Quay Bottle Company and the Wear Glass Bottle Works were but two large firms in the area. The Corning Glass factory now stands on the site of the Shoulder of Mutton.

The Wavendon, Wavendon Crescent
Above: The Wavendon opened on 7th August 1959, having taken nine months to build at a cost of £30,000. *Left and right:* Staff from the Wavendon today.

The Chesters, Chester Road

Right: This pub began life as a vicarage. The foundation stone had been laid in 1869 by the daughter of the vicar of St. Mark's. Vaux & Co. bought the vicarage with the intention to develop it as a hotel. During the Second World War the brewery let the building to the Corporation as a children's day nursery. In 1944 a proposal was put forward to transfer the licence of the Saltgrass to the former vicarage, as well as sacrifice an off licence in Chester Road. When the war ended they planned to build a new hotel on the site, to be named The Chesters, at a cost of £25,000 to £30,000. The application, however, was rejected by the Licensing Magistrates. A licence was eventually granted for The Chesters in 1954, but only then as a pub converted from the vicarage. In recent years plans have been put forward to demolish the Chesters and rebuild it nearer the main road but these have been rejected.

The Winston, Hanover Place

Above: While The Winston has only been a pub since the 1980s, the building in which it is housed is much older. The pub is converted from a shipyard directors' launch room.

Fitzgeralds, Green Terrace

This bar has recently changed its name from Greensleeves but the building itself has a much longer history. It is one of the few eighteenth century buildings to have survived in Sunderland. At one time it was owned by a Quaker family, the Richardsons. They owned the nearby tanyard and flour mill. In the last century many pubs were converted from dwelling houses, later when pubs began to be made redundant the process was reversed. In the *Sunderland Daily Echo* of 8th July 1912 three former pubs appeared in an advert for up coming auctions. These were the Ferry Hotel, Low Street; the Brown Jug, Adelaide Street, Southwick and the Windsor Castle, Zetland Street, Monkwearmouth.

Law and Enforcement

In the period before the establishment of the Borough Police Force in 1837, responsibility for keeping law and order in the town lay in the hands of Churchwardens and Parish Constables. Records survive of the receipts and expenses of the Churchwarden and Constables in the early nineteenth century. These include:

19th April 1828 To two Constables apprehending Keeping in Custody and Putting in the Stocks John Rennison for being drunk and disorderly 5-0d

As well as powers to arrest lawbreakers such as drunks, Parish Constables were responsible for the surveillance of licences for taverns.

23rd February 1823 Two Constables going about the Lanes on Sunday amongst the Public Houses 10-0d

In *Old Monkwearmouth and its Surroundings: Seventy Years Ago* (1892), John Thompson recalled how Churchwardens used to call at the Nag's Head in Whitburn Street, after the church service had begun to make sure the law was not broken. They were then given the best the house could offer, all free of charge. Thompson recalled how, "whenever the name of the Churchwarden was mentioned, it seemed to strike into the youthful minds much more than the name of a policeman of the present day".

After Robert Peel established the Metropolitan Police Force in 1829, it was only a matter of time before Sunderland had its own Force, and this came in November 1837.

The new Police Force had an immediate impact not only on drinkers but also on those who sold alcohol. On 2nd December 1837, eleven men were fined for being drunk and disorderly and eleven publicans and beerhouse keepers were fined. Their offences included, allowing gambling on licensed premises and 'suffering tippling' in their house during divine service.

One local councillor took up the publicans' cause and raised the matter in the Town Council in February 1838. Councillor Walker complained that the police were treating landlords harshly, by 'carrying on a system of espionage'. This deterred many people from visiting pubs, which in turn damaged the pub owner's legitimate business. Walker cited the case of one respectable landlord, who was fined for playing a game of cards with his own family.

In 1783 Sunderland Parish Vestry had a lock-up or cage built in Coronation Street, nicknamed 'The Kitty' *(below)*. Not far from this stood the Parish stocks. In the Kitty there was a small window with an iron grating, through which relatives and friends of the prisoner passed whisky and food. The vast majority of its temporary inmates were drunks, some of whom were taken to the courts in High Street by wheelbarrow. The Police inherited the Kitty as well as one in Monkwearmouth which stood on Cage Hill. While on nearby Look Out Hill stood Monkwearmouth stocks. John Thompson recalled seeing one famous local, Tommy Crommy, placed in these stocks for being drunk. While fighting under Nelson, Crommy had lost both his legs. After the constable was satisfied his prisoner was securely installed in the stocks he left. Crommy then unstrapped his wooden legs and set himself free to roars of laughter from the assembled crowd.

The quality of policemen in the early years of the force was not of a high quality. At this time police were poorly paid and free drink was seen as a perk of the job. Out of the first 35 men to join Sunderland Police Force, 22 were dismissed, most for drinking on duty. The problems caused by drink were seen right through to the end of the century. Between 10th February 1897 and 10th May 1899 14 Sunderland policemen were disciplined by the Watch Committee for drink-related offences. Six men were dismissed from the force and eight reduced in rank. Their offences included, 'being drunk on duty', 'found drinking on licensed premises', 'brought off duty the worse for liquor' and in one instance, 'being drunk on licensed premises whilst off duty'. The Watch Committee reports were recorded in the Council Minutes. These included the following cases:

> 14th April 1897 'reported that they had reduced Sub-Inspector Atkinson to the rank of Sergeant for neglecting his duty, by being in the "Hat and Feather" Public House, on the 18th February last'

> 9th March 1898 'dismissed P.C. 59 Joseph Armstrong, from the Force for being brought off duty the worse for liquor, using insubordinate language, and threatening Sergeant Murray'

The police were not popular with the majority of the population in the middle of the last century. Whenever the opportunity arose, such as the arrests of drunks, they showed their derision for the force. The military stationed in town on occasions also did not see eye to eye with the police.

On 14th April 1838 two soldiers on recruiting duty in High Street were talking to a potential recruit when they were pushed by a policeman and told to move on. After a scuffle the soldier was arrested but a crowd rescued him. The recruiting party then went to a pub and when they emerged they were greeted with cheers from the large gathering. Caps and hats were thrown in the air and a truncheon taken from the police held high. There were cries of 'Down with the police' from the estimated one thousand onlookers, as the soldiers marched back to the barracks.

Later in court there were conflicting stories as to how the trouble started. The wife of a Corporal Owen was said to have been pushed in the back of the neck by a police officer. Lewis, one of the accused soldiers, said the policeman was drunk at the time. An allegation strongly denied. The Magistrates found three soldiers guilty and fined two of them 20s and the other 40s and costs.

A far more serious disturbance between soldiers and the police occurred ten years later. It started when a soldier from the 63rd (Irish) Regiment stationed in town, was going to fight a sailor. A policeman intervened and after a struggle Private Thompson was arrested as well as a soldier called Jordan who tried to help him escape.

The next day, Saturday 23rd September 1848, they were found guilty by the Magistrates and fined 20s. On the same day groups of soldiers began to gather in Low Street. Then thirty soldiers attacked a number of policemen with belts and handkerchiefs filled with glasses and bottles. Inspector Temple was knocked unconscious in an entry to Wylam's Wharf. He was carried into the Jim Crow public house, which in turn was attacked by soldiers. Hundreds of people watched events unfold and many, including navvies employed in the New Docks, joined in on the side of the soldiers. The siege of the Jim Crow ended with the arrival of a detail from the barracks. Peace was then restored and the following day (Sunday) was quiet, but on the Monday events took a further twist. At 11 o'clock in the morning the Mayor, Mr. Kitson, Superintendent Brown and a number of witnesses went to the barracks to identify the soldiers involved.

After inspecting some troops, the 7th Company stormed out of their rooms brandishing bayonets and swinging belts overhead, and charged at the group of civilians. At this point the Mayor's party turned tail and ran out of the barrack gates. The *Sunderland Herald* of 29th September reported the scene:

> Some lost their shoes, others their hats, one an umbrella, and another had his trouser legs nearly torn off. Among those who lost their hats was Sergeant Bell, whose cape as he came flying along, in a slouching posture, was raised aloft by "the wind of his own speed" in such a manner that one of several women who, alarmed by the uproar, had thrown up their windows to look out, actually shouted in great trepidation, "O L --! there's a man running without his head.

The Mayor immediately sent a statement to Home Secretary, Sir George Grey. The next day (Tuesday) Colonel Pole arrived and the following day the three companies were transferred to Newcastle and replaced. In a court case the following October, five soldiers were charged with the original attack on the police. Three of these were found guilty and fined £5.

Jim Crow.

ESTABLISHMENT,
Foot of Stob-Lane, Low Street,
SUNDERLAND,

For the Sale of Foreign and British Wines, Foreign and British Spirits, Meux and Co.'s Entire London Porter in Casks and Bottles, Genuine Ale of all kinds, Cordials, &c. &c.

CHARLTON BEWICK & Co. beg most respectfully to inform their Friends and the Public, that in opening the above Establishment they have laid in a choice Stock of Articles of the above description, which they intend to sell over the Counter by Retail, at the lowest possible Prices for Ready Money, and from the experience of the Party who selected them, they defy competition either in Price or Quality.

JAMAICA RUM.—Knowing from experience that Age only can give to Rums that softness and richness of flavour for which they are so justly admired, C. B. and Co. have selected only such, and which they can confidently recommend.

GIN.—They have much pleasure in recommending the produce of their own Country, English Gin, which is now brought to the highest state of perfection; it is vatted and will be found a soft and pure Spirit.

BRANDY.—C. B. and Co. being anxious not to be rivalled in this valuable Article, are determined to keep a large Stock on hand of the best Marks, to secure an old and choice Spirit.

WHISKY.—Having laid in a Stock of the celebrated Islay and Highland Whiskys, which are seldom sold in this part of the Country, they particularly call the attention of their Friends and the Public to them.

FOREIGN WINES.—Port varies so much in flavour and quality that it is difficult to please all palates, but C. B. and Co. trust they have made such an extensive selection, that they cannot do otherwise than gratify the most fastidious Connoisseur. The same may be said of all their other Wines, viz.—Sherry, Champagne, Claret, Hock, Madeira, "London Particular," &c. &c. Port and Sherry sold from the Wood by the Quart.

BRITISH WINES.—So much used in Private Families. Every attention has been paid to them, and they can strongly recommend their Ginger, Elderberry, Raspberry, Orange, and other Wines.

LONDON PORTER.—Meux and Co.'s Entire, C. B. and Co. are determined the Public shall have a treat in their Genuine London Porter, either in Cask or Bottle.

ALE.—It is generally acknowledged that Malt Liquors, if obtained in a pure and genuine state, are a wholesome and nutritious beverage, C. B. and Co. have therefore got some prepared for this Establishment only, which they can offer as a really Genuine Article.

Publicans and others *particularly situated* will find this Establishment well worthy of their notice, the Proprietors being determined to sell at the lowest possible Price for Cash. Private Families will also find it their interest to patronize this Establishment.

C. B. and Co. also beg to state, that they have fitted up in the best style several Rooms for the reception of Private Parties, where every attention will be paid to those who may favour them with their Company.

DINNERS ON THE SHORTEST NOTICE.

Low Street, Sunderland, foot of Stob-lane, August 24th, 1838.

REED AND SON, PRINTERS, SUNDERLAND.

An advert for the Jim Crow, at which the police took refuge from the soldiers. The Low Street pub was later renamed The Propeller.

Ship Inn, Portobello Lane
This inn stood on a small lane off Broad Street (later Roker Avenue) in the middle of the last century. *Above*: A sketch of the Ship Inn in 1840. At this time the proprietor was Mr. Robson.

Shipwrights' Arms, Dame Dorothy Street
This old pub was known as the 'Duzzy House'. Possibly because the especially strong beer on sale there made drinkers duzzy (dizzy).

The Look Out, Millum Terrace
This pub took its name from nearby Look Out Hill. The 'hill' had been formed of ballast sand dumped from ships arriving on the Wear. There were four of these ballast hills in Monkwearmouth, the furthest east and therefore overlooking the harbour, being Look Out Hill. After closing as a pub the Look Out was used as a club for unemployed men.

The Grange, Newcastle Road
Above: One of the more modern pubs in Sunderland, The Grange stands at an old crossroads. In the last century it linked the villages of Southwick and Fulwell and it was the main route between Sunderland and Newcastle.

Williamson Arms, Church Street
Above: This nineteenth century public house bore the name of Monkwearmouth's most famous family. Sir Hedworth Williamson at one time owned virtually all of the land between Whitburn and the River Wear. The Zetland Arms was another pub with a Williamson family connection in its name. The Williamson Arms consisted of a Long Bar, Tap Room, Front and Back Parlours and had its own quoit ground in the back.

Sheet Anchor, Dundas Street
Former Sunderland and England footballer, Warney Cresswell (*above*) managed this popular pub after his playing days were over. *Left:* The pub closed in the 1960s and the building demolished.

Wolseley Hotel, Millum Terrace
In the 1970s one of the regulars, Tommy the Greek had his dog barred by the pub's landlord. The terrier, was often encouraged by Tommy's cronies to attack the Wolseley's curtains. This happened once too often and the dog was refused entry.

The Vulcan, Millum Terrace
In 1861 the Vulcan was run by James Carling. After more than a hundred years in business the Vulcan was forced to close for redevelopment.

Newcastle Arms, Monkwearmouth
One of the earliest references to a public house on the north bank of the Wear concerned the Newcastle Arms. The *Newcastle Courant* of 9th June 1792 reported the death the previous Thursday "after a lingering illness, Mr. John Hepple, Keeper of the Newcastle Arms, Monkwearmouth."

Jack Crawford, Whitburn Street
This nineteenth century pub was named after the Sunderland-born 'Hero of Camperdown'. It met its end in an air raid during the last war *(left)*. The figure depicting Crawford climbing the mast to nail the colours back (to the left of the pub sign) can now be seen in Sunderland Museum.

During the early part of the last century cock fighting was popular in Monkwearmouth and there was a Fighting Cock Inn in Thomas Street. The inn had a whale bone sign, on one side stood two fighting cocks before a fight and on the reverse a dying cock with its victor. The owner, John Taylor went bankrupt and in 1809 the Fighting Cock was sold. After this the pub was renamed the Freemasons' Tavern because the St. Paul Lodge of Monkwearmouth Freemasons held their meetings there. One of the main patrons of cock fighting was Squire John Stafford of Fort House. One of Stafford's fellow enthusiasts was Bill Bainbridge, landlord of The Artichoke public house.

Borough Hotel, Yorke Street
Left: The Borough in Yorke Street like its namesake across the river got its name from the Borough of Sunderland. In the 1850s the Borough's licensees were the Latham family, first Michael and then Hannah. When the pub was put up for sale in 1891 it was advertised as having "Large Front Sitting Bar with Plate-Glass Frontage, Front Sitting Room, Back Bar Snug and Private and Public Sitting Rooms".

Red Lion, Roker Avenue

The original Red Lion dated from at least 1827 at which time George Bainsby was landlord. This was in John Street which lay at the top end of Broad Street. After Broad Street was widened in the last century (forming Roker Avenue) the Red Lion was rebuilt on the site of what had been the stable yard of the Brandling Hotel.

Right: The Red Lion is still one of the most popular pubs in the area. On match days it is a rendezvous for supporters on route to Roker Park.

Above: Irene and Ann (*on the right of picture*) behind the bar in the Red Lion. Ann and Tony Smith are the present licensees. Sunderland-born Tony, maintains a long tradition of ex-professional footballers in the licensing trade. After playing for West Ham United, Watford and Hartlepool he started a new career in his hometown.

The Red Lion, a traditional pub: a place for drinking....

.... conversation .... and contemplation.

The Fort, Roker Avenue
One of only a handful of nineteenth century pubs to survive in Monkwearmouth. This was thanks mainly to its location on Roker Avenue which escaped the major post war redevelopment. The pub took its name from its location on Fort Hill. At one time a windmill had stood on the site.

Howard Arms, Roker Avenue
This is another pub which benefits from match day custom. One of the pub's landlords earlier in the century met an unfortunate end. William Wilkinson had worked as a plater in the shipyards before becoming a licensee. In 1928 after leaving the pub he found work on the construction of the new Wearmouth Bridge. On the morning of 24th September a steel girder slipped while being lifted and fatally struck the 39-year-old former Howard Arms landlord.

Wearmouth Bridge, Thomas Street
In 1827 this appears in *Pigot's Directory* as the Sunderland Bridge. By 1834 it was known as the Wearmouth Bridge which it remained for over a century (*above left*). After it closed it stood empty for a time before becoming an Indian restaurant. In 1979 it reopened as a public house (*above right*), with the new name of The Terminus (a bus company has a depot facing).

Blue Bell Hotel, Roker Avenue

The old Blue Bell which stood on Broad Street had as its landlord in 1827 Timothy Tooley.

In 1894 plans were put forward to rebuild the aging inn. At the Annual Licensing meeting the proposal was opposed by the nearby Monkwearmouth and Southwick Hospital, whose representative Mr. Nicholson declared, "there was already abundant accommodation in the neighbourhood for the purchase of liquor, as within a radius of 250 yards of the inn there were no fewer than 16 licensed houses". The local vicar, Reverend Hancock also feared increased drunkenness in the area if the licence was granted. The licence was refused

After a number of further unsuccessful attempts at a provisional licence for a new Blue Bell it was finally granted in 1900. The new building was an impressive feature of the Monkwearmouth landscape until the night of the 7th November 1941 when it was wrecked by a German bomb (*bottom right*). Things could have been much worse as the raid occurred shortly after closing time and there was only the manager, manageress and one barmaid in the building at the time and they all escaped serious injury. In February 1942, the Licensing Magistrates gave approval for rebuilding. At the time the owners Newcastle Breweries could not go ahead immediately and the new Blue Bell never did get built.

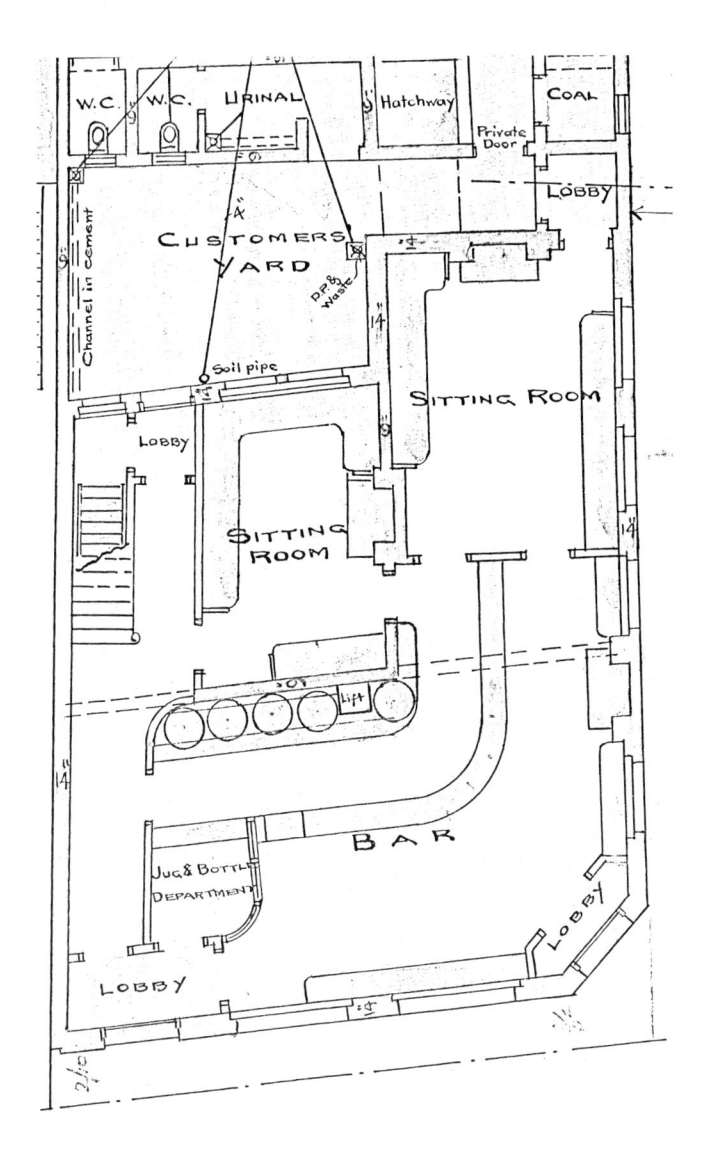

Above and left: Architect's plans for the Blue Bell which were finally granted in 1900.

Wheatsheaf Hotel, Roker Avenue

The Wheatsheaf was one of the oldest coaching inns north of the river. In 1827 the 'Lion' coach left from here every morning at 10 a.m. for South Shields and returned at 5 p.m. By 1834 the owner, John Crowe was advertising "a gig nearly every hour to Shields for passengers". This trade was severely hit with the introduction of the railways. The Wheatsheaf was also an important meeting place in the days when the surrounding area was comprised mainly of farmland. During the harvest season the inn was where farmers hired hands to cut their crops. Among these seasonal labourers were groups of women with formidable reputations known as the 'Shearers'. *Above:* A busy scene at the Wheatsheaf at the end of the last century.

The original Wheatsheaf.

The present Wheatsheaf dating from early this century.

Barrington Hotel, Millum Terrace
The Barrington stood on the corner of Millum Terrace and Barrington Street and like many neighbouring pubs was demolished in the 1960s.

DERBY HOTEL,

Millum Terrace, Roker.

C. W. FRYERS, Proprietor.

VISITORS TO ROKER should call at this FREE HOUSE,
NOTED for the Quality of its

MILD AND BITTER ALES.

The Best that an Open Market can produce.

Wines, Spirits, Cigars, etc.
"The Best of Everything is good enough for anybody."

Derby Hotel, Millum Terrace
The location of this hotel meant it had a view of both the Wear and Roker. In 1890 it was put up for sale. It was advertised as having a Bar, Front and Back Snugs, two Sitting Rooms, Bottling Cellar, Washroom and a large cemented yard. The private apartment comprised four large rooms. The premises were bought for the sum of £2,725, which did not include gas fittings, spirit barrels and '6-motion Beer machine' which were extra. *Top right*: An advert for the Derby from 1905. The Derby was demolished in the redevelopment of Millum Terrace in the early 1960s. *Bottom right*: The New Derby in Roker Baths Road which opened in 1963 ensured the name continued.

Hope Tavern, Dixon Square
Left: This pub lay in a small square formerly called The Curtain which lies just off Roker Avenue, beside the Howard Arms. The Hope dated from the early part of the last century and closed its doors for the last time on 8th November 1960. Unlike many of its neighbours redevelopment work did not force the Hope's closure. It was shut under a scheme which redistributed licensed premises to meet the increasing need for pubs in the newly emerging housing estates on the edge of town. Today, Smudgers night club *(above)* now occupies the site of the old Hope Tavern.

Pear Tree, Hardwicke Street
There had at one time been a much older Pear Tree in Monkwearmouth but this stood in Strand Street near Look Out Hill. The Pear Tree in Hardwicke Street was a beerhouse that was known to locals as the 'Old Boat'. One explanation for the origin of this name was the fact the pub was a meeting place for ships crews and wages were shared out in the bar.

In 1932 the police tried to close the Pear Tree on the grounds it was surplus to requirements. Superintendent Cook disclosed to the Licensing Sessions that the police had kept watch on the premises. He said "we were there about half-an-hour, and no one came in expect a kiddie to ask the time". It was disclosed that the weekly takings of the Pear Tree was £25, of which £2. 15s. was paid to the landlord and his wife. The lack of trade and the fact there were seven other pubs within 250 yards was the police's argument to revoke the licence. On 2nd March 1932 the magistrates decided to renew the licence; thus delaying last orders at the 'Old Boat' for another thirty years.

Star Brewery, Dixon Square
The Star Brewery was one of the numerous small breweries on Wearside in the last century. *Left:* The building and its sign *(above)* survive today. The former brewery is now a garage.

Victor Hotel, Victor Street
The Victor was so small the dart board was behind the bar and the doors had to be locked during a darts match. A boarded-up Victor Hotel shortly before its demolition (*above*). Its life might have been shorter still, if one of the Victor's owners had his way it would have closed in 1898. At the Licensing Sessions on 25th August of that year, Jack Clough sought a full license for a new house to be built on the site of the Blue Bell in Roker Avenue. As a 'sweetener' to the Magistrates, Clough offered to give up the license of another of his pubs: The Victor Hotel. However, this was tuned down by the Magistrates and the Victor survived.

The Grapes, Dundas Street
In *Old Monkwearmouth and its Surroundings: Seventy Years Ago* (1892) John Thompson recorded how The Grapes was built in 1826 by Thomas Walker. It was built on a site that had formerly been gardens and orchards. The 1820-22 *Commercial Directory* records a Grapes public house already in Monkwearmouth, run by a Jacob Wilkinson. The Grapes in Dundas Street was finally demolished in the 1980s.

White Swan, Williamson Street
At the White Swan on 29th May, 1823 the Monkwearmouth Shipwright's Union Society was founded. At the time shipbuilding was a major employer in the area and the White Swan was one of dozens of pubs that flourished. The White Swan was known to Barbary Coasters as 'The Shanty'.

Marquis of Lorne, Millum Terrace
Left: In the 1960s the Marquis kept a slate for regulars, many of whom were shipyard workers, who settled up on pay day. If any man could not pay and deliberately avoided seeing the landlady, his name was displayed in the bar for all to see.

Princess of Wales, Millum Terrace
This pub stood on the corner of Millum Terrace and Hardwicke Street opposite the Vulcan. At one time there were seven pubs in Millum Terrace. Of these, only the Wolseley remains open today.

Aquatic Arms, North Bridge Street
A view of the Aquatic through the bridge linking Monkwearmouth Station and Wearmouth Bridge *(left)*. The Aquatic in 1973 shortly before its demolition *(above)*. At one time ex-Sunderland footballer, Arthur Housam was its manager. The Aquatic was a popular 'watering hole' for tatters (rag and bone men) who had their stables in nearby Sheepfolds. Pete Smith was one of these men and, when he had a few drinks, often took his horse in the bar with him.

Oak Tree, North Bridge Street
Early in the last century the Olde Oak Tree was the only building on the east side of North Bridge Street between Wearmouth Bridge and The Wheatsheaf. Later a new building was built on the site and remained open until the 1960s (*above*).

Engineers' Tavern, Sheepfolds Road
Left: This was known as 'Ma Vick's after Mrs. Elizabeth Vickery who ran the Engineers in the 1930s. *Above*: The last licensee, Rose Roberts behind the bar shortly before its closure in January 1971. One group who mourned its passing were the men who had pigeon lofts on the nearby banks of the Wear, as they used to hold their weekly meetings there.

Blue Bell, Fulwell Road
Above: The original Blue Bell served the small village of Fulwell in the nineteenth century. To meet growing demand this was rebuilt in 1887. When plans were made to replace this building in the 1930s it was decided to build the new pub alongside the old, thus 'maintaining continuity of license'. A novel feature of the new Blue Bell (*below*) was a garden where drinks could be served. Some of the garden seats were made from timber taken from HMS *Powerful*, a scrapped First World War ship.

Bee Hive Hotel, Barclay Street
The Bee Hive was one of the pubs that disappeared from Monkwearmouth due to either redevelopment or redundancy. Others included: The Fountain, Edinburgh House, Duke of York, Gateshead Arms and Nag's Head.

Social Tavern, Nelson Square
One of the last pubs to go in the 1960s redevelopment of the north side of the river. In keeping with the sailing and shipbuilding tradition of the area, the Social had a ship's voice pipe installed. This enabled the landlord to keep in touch when upstairs.

Engineers' Arms, Whickham Street
Right: One of the Engineers' regulars, Joe Miller could not understand why his boxer dog was falling about as if drunk. He then discovered the dog was drinking from a bucket of left over beer behind the bar.

Friendly Tavern, Yorke Street North
This was another common name for pubs on both sides of the Wear. In 1871 as well as the Friendly Tavern in Yorke Street North there was another five pubs bearing that name.

The Alexandra, Dundas Street
In 1881 this Monkwearmouth pub was owned by Longstaff and Stephenson. For years the Alexandra was known as the New Bar or Jackson's (after the owners of the late 1920s and 1930s). After major renovation the pub reopened in April 1993 with the new name of Benedict Biscop. It was named after the first Abbot of nearby St. Peter's.

Cambridge Hotel, Fulwell Road
Left: The Cambridge is one of the oldest surviving pubs north of the river, dating from 1871. At this time Nicholas Prior was the landlord.

Below: Barmaid, Margaret Calvert, serving a regular in the Cambridge in modern days.

Olive Branch, Howick Street
Above: The Olive Branch was a small pub with a toilet down a steep flight of stairs. Children often used to wait until dark for a foreign sailor to descend, then a gentle push would send him down with a crash scattering loose change on the ground. Once the victim had picked himself up and found his money there would always be some coins missed for the kids to take.

The Albion, Dock Street East
Above: In 1865 John Cunningham was landlord of this pub which has survived the redevelopment of the area.

Clipper Ship, Victor Street
In 1865 the Clipper Ship (*above*) was run by Thomas Smart. It had been named after the tea clippers which were built in the neighbouring shipyards. One of these ships, The Torrens gave its name to a pub of its own a century later. *Above right:* The bar of the Clipper Ship in the 1950s, popular with the nearby North Sands shipyard workers. The 1960s saw the Clipper Ship's closure, but a new pub bearing the name opened in nearby Zetland Street (*right*). This was built on the site of Lautebach's mineral water works. In November 1968 this was taken over by Sunderland Football Supporters Club as its headquarters. After only a few years it reverted back to an ordinary pub. It is still open having shortened its name to The Clipper.

Royal Hotel, North Bridge Street
Built in the middle of the last century the Royal was only demolished in 1973. *Above left:* The Royal in the last century when it was owned by Richardsons. The architect, Thomas Moore, also designed the nearby Monkwearmouth Railway Station which still stands today. The Royal did survive air raids of the Second World War. On 9th August, 1940 a bomb landed on the nearby railway bridge over Sheepfolds Road but damage was limited to broken windows. *Above right:* The derelict building shortly before its demolition.

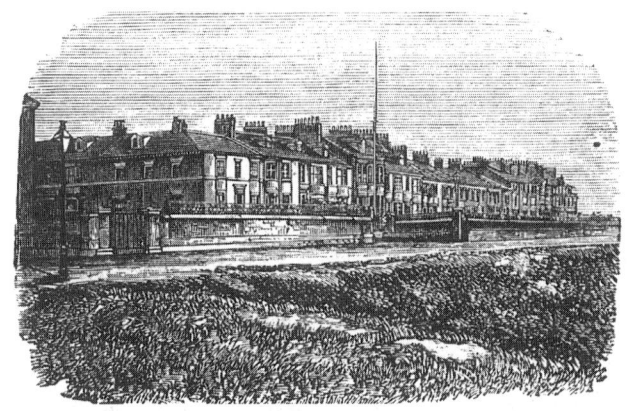

CHARGES.

Victuals, £1 8s. per week; Ditto in Private Room, £1 18s. 6d.; Bed Rooms, from 8s. to 12s. ditto; Double Bedded Rooms, from 12s. to 16s. do.; Private Sitting ditto, 12s. to 15s. ditto; Fires in Sitting and Bed Rooms, 3s. 6d. per week; Sitting Room and Bed Room under a week, from 5s. per day. Persons not having Apartments, nor taking their Victuals regularly:— Breakfast, 2s.; Dinner, 2s. 6d.; Tea, 1s. 6d. each Person; Bed and Breakfast, £1 1s. per week. *The above include Chambermaid, Waiter, Boots, and Attendance of every description.*

CHARGES FOR BATHING.

Before 10 o'clock in the Morning, and after 4 in the Afternoon:—

Warm Bath	1s 6d	Warm Shower Bath	9d
Cold do.	1s 0d	Cold do. do.	6d

Between the above-named hours, charges are:—

Warm Bath	2s 0d	Vapour Bath	2s 6d
Cold do.	1s 0d	Shower do.	0s 9d

Use of Sea Bathing Machine, 3d.; if taken into the Sea with a Horse, 6d.
Dinners provided for Parties on the shortest notice.
Good Stabling and Coach Houses.

Roker Hotel, Roker Terrace

The hotel and baths on the Roker seafront were built in 1842 (*above left*). This comprised: two dwelling houses adjoining the bath house and stables and coach house. *Above right:* An advert for the Roker Bath Hotel from the 1844 *Vint and Carr Directory* showing the list of charges. In 1902 the resort had increased in popularity to the point the Roker Hotel (Baths had been dropped from the title) was claiming Roker as the 'Brighton of the North' (*below*). Attractions in the hotel at this time included: billiards, smoking and news rooms and buffet. *Bottom:* Today, the Roker Hotel remains one of the area's most popular pubs, both with locals and visitors.

William Pile, Dame Dorothy Street and Zetland Street
Right: This pub was named after one of Sunderland's most famous shipbuilders of the nineteenth century. Pile's shipyards bridged the era between wood sailing ships and iron ships *Below right:* An advert from *Marwood's Maritime Directory* 1854. The yards gave work to many men in Monkwearmouth, at one time over 3,000 were employed.

During the early part of the last century Monkwearmouth rivalled the East End in the number of riverside pubs. Wear Street was a smaller version of Low Street across the river. This was an age when the port was thriving and taverns vied for the custom of seaman, keel and shipyard workers. In 1827 there were 17 pubs in Wear Street. These were; Bull and Dog, Cobble, Commercial Tavern, Ferryboat Landing House, Greenland Fishery, Keel, Oak Tree, Star and Garter, Yarmouth Arms, Monkwearmouth Brewery, Ship Clara, as well as two Aberdeen Arms, two Red Lions and Two 'Board' inns.

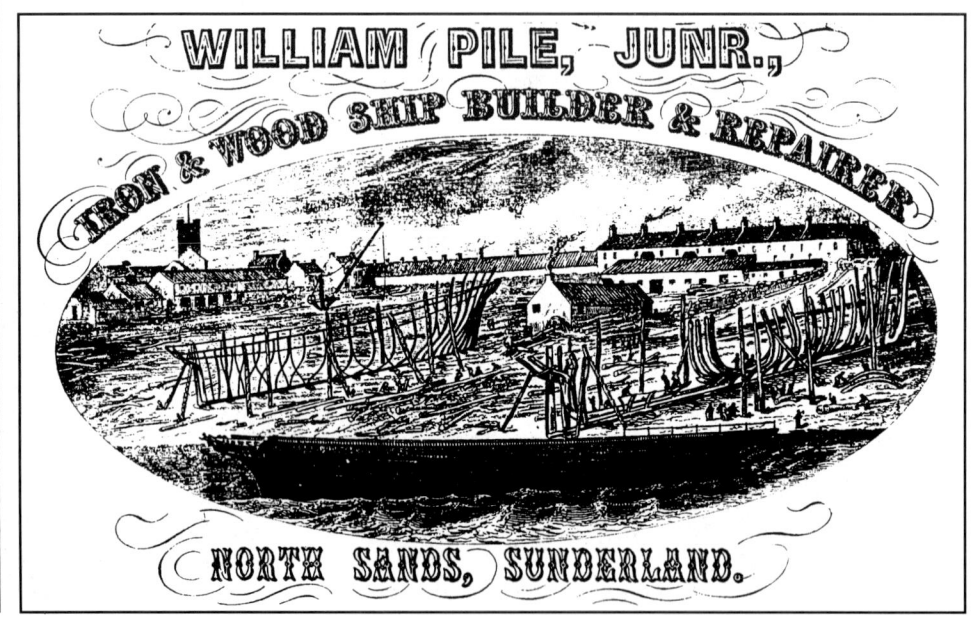

Reform Tavern, Whitburn Street
In 1841 this tavern was the scene of a riot which ended with the building ransacked and the manager in jail. On 17th September, Sunderland's newly elected Member of Parliament, Lord Howick led a victory procession through Monkwearmouth. The election campaign had been dirty with the defeated Tory, Wolverly Attwood being accused of attempting to bribe voters. As Howick's procession reached Whitburn Street they found blue and white flags (Attwood's colours) hanging from the Reform Tavern. As the procession was passing, stones were thrown from the pub into the crowd. When they retaliated in kind the landlord, Edward Liddle appeared at a first floor window brandishing a gun. He took aim at the crowd and while the gun flashed it did not discharge a shot. The crowd, incensed at this action, stormed the building and completely ransacked the bar. Liddle was arrested and taken into custody before the mob could seize him.

The following day he appeared before Magistrates charged with having "feloniously attempted to fire a loaded gun at Viscount Howick on the preceding day, with intent to do some grievous bodily harm". If found guilty Liddle faced the prospect of being transported for life. It was revealed that a number of men in the Reform Tavern at the time had been employed by the losing candidate during the election campaign. After a three day adjournment the Mayor gave the verdict; "in our opinion ... the charge of felony is not proved; at the same time he has been guilty of a most violent and outrageous assault and had it not been for the damage he has received and the loss he has sustained, in all probability we should have sent the case to the quarter sessions." Instead Liddle was fined £5 and had to find two sureties of £25 each to keep the peace for twelve months. Shortly after Liddle moved across the river and took over the Mechanics' Arms in High Street.

The Pineapple, Charles Street
George Benson, landlord of the Pineapple in 1861 was also a ship's chandler. *Left:* The Pineapple in the 1950s.

Golden Fleece, Dock Street
When this nineteenth century pub applied to renew its licence in 1932 the police objected. This was the time of the Depression and the police cited the pub's poor takings which in the year ending 31st March 1931 amounted to £2,259: an average £43 a week. By 1932 takings were down to £38 a week. Police also opposed on the grounds that there were seven drinking houses within 250 yards of the premises. The owners suggested to the Magistrates they would give up the licence of another of their houses if the Golden Fleece was renewed. Despite this offer, on the 2nd March 1932 the licence was refused and the pub was reported for compensation.

In 1913 the Rose Line bought Wylam Wharf from French & Co. *Above*: The company's old warehouses.

Above: Ships from the Rose Line loading whisky in Scotland during the 1950s.

The Alexandra, Clockwell Street
This old beerhouse had Samuel Johnson as its landlord in 1871. After surviving for more than a century the Alex was demolished in the 1960s.

This 'off' licence stood next to the Friendly Tavern in Southwick Road. Ben Ewe was a local brand of whisky. In 1861, Chancellor of the Exchequer, William Gladstone introduced a 'grocer's licence'. This allowed any shop to obtain a licence for off consumption of spirits and wines and from 1863 beer.

Colliery Tavern, Wayman Street
Named after the nearby Wearmouth Colliery this pub survived the Hood Street redevelopment of the late 1970s. In the Sheepfolds area behind the colliery up to North Bridge Street there were a number of pubs which have long since gone. In the last century these included the Sheepfolds Tavern, Fitzroys' and the Ropery Tavern. While in this century, apart from Ma Vick's in Sheepfolds Road, there were the Colliery House, the Richmond Hotel and The Waggon Tavern.

Cricketers' Arms, Pilgrim Street
On 8th May 1896 the Cricketers' was offered for sale at auction at the Royal Hotel. The property consisted of a Bar, two Snugs and a Sitting Room. Bidding started at £600 but when it had reached only £1,300 it was withdrawn. The Cricketers' was demolished in the redevelopment of the Hood Street-Pilgrim Street area in the late 1970s.

Ye Olde Friendly Tavern, Southwick Road
Right: The 'olde worlde' sounding pub went by the shortened version of Friendly Tavern. The last landlord of the Friendly was Brian Armstrong. In 1964 the building was demolished.

> **Banks of the Wear, King Street**
> This nineteenth century pub retained its gas lighting from the Victoria era right through to the 1950s. Even when it was converted to electricity the pub was still not connected to the mains, it had its own generator.

Shipwrights' Arms, Ferryboat Lane
Above: As its name implies, the Shipwrights' Arms dates from an era when the riverbank at North Hylton was industrialized. In 1854 there was half a dozen shipyards in the area, including Lister and Bartrams (later to become the famous Bartram & Sons). At this time John Stothard was landlord of the Shipwrights'. Today, the pub is still going strong but the shipyards have long since gone.

> On 18th July 1856 the *Sunderland Herald* reported, John Stonehouse, a shipwright appeared before the County Petty Sessions charged with being drunk and disorderly at Southwick. He told the court he liked his drink: "it makes me talk when I get a pot or two of porter". When he was ordered to find two sureties to keep the peace for six months, he replied "two sureties! I'll get fifty - I'll get a hundred".

Albion Hotel, Southwick Road
Left: The Albion in the 1930s. Like its neighbour, the Half Way House, the Albion has survived the clearances of the 1960s.

Wellington Tavern, Wellington Street
This was one of the most popular pubs in Southwick. The Welly was another pub that disappeared from the area in the 1960s.

Tram Car Inn, Southwick Green
The Tram Car was converted from a much older building (possibly eighteenth century). *Above:* The Tram Car today.

Sun Inn, Southwick Road
In 1834 the Sun Inn's landlord was Isaac Golightly. In 1908 the pub was put up for sale. At the auction in the Queen's Hotel bidding started at £4,000 and when it reached £8,100 it was withdrawn. However, immediately after the auction the pub was sold to James Deuchar for the sum of £8,500 (a huge sum at that time).

Castletown Inn, Castletown View
The Castletown cost £2,000 to build in the last century. Recently the pub has been renamed the Crown and Anchor.

Times Inn, Wear Street

Above: Some of the locals pose in front of the Times Inn at the turn of the century. After the First World War the Times closed and the building was put to various uses. The neighbouring Pickersgill's shipyard eventually acquired the building and used it as a store. In the 1980s after having been derelict for a number of years, the old Times Inn was rebuilt (*left*), eventually opening for business under its original name (*below*).

The Station, Stoney Lane
Above: This nineteenth century pub was known to locals as Tates. William Tate had been the licensee from the early 1860s until the 1880s. In the late 1960s the Station was demolished.

General Havelock, Stoney Lane
This eighteenth century pub was rebuilt in 1904. The General Havelock went by the name Hogans, after a former licensee. This has now become the pub's official name (*above*).

North Star, Kings Road
Right: In 1876 the old North Star was put up for sale. The pub was part of the estate of the late John Wandless. Included with the North Star was a double cottage adjoining a quoit ground and four cottages behind. Bidding started at £1,500 and the whole lot finally went for £2,505. Major reconstruction later changed the frontage to its present day rounded shape (*above right*). At the end of 1981 after another refurbishment the pub reopened with a new name 'The Sheltered Deck'. This was after the SD 14 cargo ships built at the Southwick Shipyards. However, it was pointed out that SD stood for 'shelter deck' and it was renamed thus in January 1982.

Smiths' Arms, Southwick Green   **Old Mill, Southwick Green**

These two pubs were built in the 1820s. Standing only a few yards apart, they were also demolished only a few years apart in the 1980s. The property between the pubs was a blacksmith during the last century. After the closure of the Smiths' Arms, Councillor Hall tried to save the building as part of Southwick's heritage. His efforts failed and in 1984 suffered the same fate as the Old Mill which was demolished three years before.

> Shipbuilding and glassmaking were two industries that flourished on the riverside at Southwick in the last century. To meet the needs of these workers dozens of pubs sprang up. These included: Pedestrian Arms, Victoria Street; Park Hotel, Wear Street and Sportsman's Inn, King Street.

Mill House Inn, Southwick Road
Above: This pub is known to locals as the 'Half Way House' from its position, during the last century, midway between the villages of Monkwearmouth and Southwick. After Sunderland's FA Cup win in 1973, the landlord at that time, John Brian Armstrong had the building painted red and white (*above right*).

Black Cat Publications

(091) 564 2445

Old Pubs of Sunderland
Volume Two
by
Alan Brett

Old Pubs of Sunderland
Volume Two
£4.99